THE EMPEROR'S ORPHANS

THE EMPEROR'S ORPHANS

by

Sally Ito

TURNSTONE PRESS

Turnstone Press
Artspace Building
206-100 Arthur Street
Winnipeg, MB
R3B 1H3 Canada
www.TurnstonePress.com

MIX
Paper from
responsible sources
FSC® C016245

Turnstone Press gratefully acknowledges the assistance of the Canada Council for the Arts, the Manitoba Arts Council, the Government of Canada, and the Province of Manitoba through the Book Publishing Tax Credit and the Book Publisher Marketing Assistance Program.

Cover photographs: Shōwa Emperor (Hirohito) at his enthronement in 1928, commons. wikimedia.org/wiki/File:Emperor_Showa.jpg / Ito boys, Lemon Creek, photo courtesy Sally Ito.

Printed and bound in Canada by Friesens.

This book is a memoir and reflects the author's experiences as they have recalled them. Names, events, dialogue and characterizations may have been changed, compressed or recreated for the purposes of telling their story.

Library and Archives Canada Cataloguing in Publication

Ito, Sally, 1964-, author
    The emperor's orphans / Sally Ito.

Issued in print and electronic formats.

ISBN 978-0-88801-567-9 (softcover).--ISBN 978-0-88801-568-6 (EPUB).--
ISBN 978-0-88801-569-3 (Kindle).--ISBN 978-0-88801-570-9 (PDF)

    1. Ito, Sally, 1964-. 2. Ito, Sally, 1964- --Family. 3. Authors,Canadian (English)-
-20th century--Biography. 4. Japanese Canadians--Biography. 5. Japanese Canadi-
ans--Evacuation and relocation, 1942-1945. 6. Autobiographies. I. Title.

PS8567.T63Z46 2018   C813'.54   C2018-904639-2
                                                C2018-904640-6

MANITOBA ARTS COUNCIL
CONSEIL DES ARTS DU MANITOBA

Canada Council   Conseil des arts
for the Arts   du Canada

Funded by the Government of Canada
Financé par le gouvernement du Canada

Canada

Manitoba

*This book is dedicated to the
Saitos and Itos of my past, present and future.*

Author's note: As this is a work of creative non-fiction, some elements are speculative and interpretive of events, and are reflections of my own thoughts and opinions about the past.

Preface

When I was in my forties, a Mennonite writer gave me a lift home from a meeting. As we were driving down the darkened elm-lined trees of my neighbourhood, we spoke about writing. At one point, I said something like, "I write to find my cultural identity." When those words came out of my mouth, it was like blurting out a truth that had remained a mystery to me all the years I had been a writer. The effect of it on my psyche was strange: I felt intense relief but also disappointment. It was like I had inflated a balloon only to have found, while tying it up, that I'd let go of the whole damn thing.

Release.

If I were a more enlightened being, I would have been freed by my words. The self-absorbed work of finding out who I was—for that, ultimately, is what a search for identity entails—could suddenly be terminated by the naming of the quest. Except, the quest wasn't over yet. Things were happening within my family that revealed ever stranger and unhappier truths about the consequences the war had on us—there was damage and loss—which would percolate through generations to me.

The people who formed me came from a rich culture of complexity and beauty. As does everyone, because culture is being enacted everywhere through rituals, traditions, performances, events, and especially in writing.

Writing was a thing I loved to do, and which I was also trained to do. The trained part of me, after years of practise, saw writing in compartmentalized categories. You wrote poetry or prose, you wrote essays or scripts. Whatever came out in words had to submit to form; this rule was a necessary discipline in my development as a writer.

But often in art, the form of something arises organically out of its creation. The writer is a lump of clay waiting to find form at the beginning of their life in language. Writing one's story is a becoming of oneself through language, and, as such, it is, as Carl Jung aptly put it in *Memories, Dreams, Reflections*, a telling of one's personal myth. A myth is the manifestation of imagined truth, and that is what *The Emperor's Orphans* is—a telling of my personal myth with some parts imagined, some parts true. It is a lump of clay now shaped and given a name to set before the reader who undertakes the journey of my tale.

—Sally Ito

THE EMPEROR'S ORPHANS

Chapter One:

My Hometown

My Hometown

My mother's hometown
is over the mountains
in a village of peach trees
where peach blossoms bloom.

My nanny's hometown
is over the ocean
on a far-off island
where seagulls flock.

My hometown—
I don't know where it is.
But I'm sure
it must be somewhere.

—Misuzu Kaneko

Taber, May 2014

We are driving down Highway 3 to Taber, Alberta, in two cars—
my sister's family in one and mine in the other—to make a short
but important side trip from our holiday visit at Waterton Lakes.
We are going to make contact with family we haven't visited in
decades. My father's people—as the old parlance would have it—
are located here and Taber is my birthplace.

As we drive through the rolling, hilly countryside, the terrain
feels unfamiliar. I may have been born in this part of the province but I have never lived here. In the distance are tall, statuesque
windmills slowly rotating their blades, harvesting the wind's invisible energies for future use. An old story told by my Nisei great-
aunt surfaces:

> It was so windy when I moved here from British
> Columbia. Every day the wind blew. I thought, "I'm
> not working in those beet fields until the wind dies

down," so I stayed inside. Finally, Papa said, "Kiyoe, you go out there and work like everyone else. The wind never stops blowing here. You just have to learn to work in it." So I went out there, and you know how you plant against the wind, Sally? You turn your butt towards it. That's what you do.

Suddenly, I hear the cackling sound of my great-aunt's laughter and see her small eyes curl up in mirth. I miss her, my beloved Auntie Kay, as we called her, using her English name. She died in February of the previous year, in Calgary, at the age of ninety-eight. Her memorial service is in Edmonton next week, and my sister and I agree to take this short holiday trip to Taber before then so our families can spend some time together.

Auntie Kay was the last of her Nisei siblings to die. Her older sister, Chiyoko, my grandmother, died in Japan in 1994 and her brother, 'Jack' Koji, died here, in southern Alberta, the same year. We are going now to visit Jack's widow, Molly, and her unmarried son, Kenny, with whom she now lives, because I would like to do what the Japanese call *ohaka mairi*. Visiting the dead.

Auntie Kay's parents—Saichi and Ei—are buried in a cemetery just outside of town. Although I do not have Kay's ashes with me, I have a framed aerial photograph of her farm in Opal, Alberta, taken in 1977. Somehow, I want to bring her land and the land her parents were buried on together into the same frame of reference. Out of that frame, I was born into this province, this country.

My baby photo album—a thick, gold-coiled affair with an embroidered cover of a fawn addressing woodland creatures in a meadow—tells of my birth on September 26, 1964 (or Showa 39, as this album is Japanese), at 10:10 in the evening. My birthplace is listed as "Canada, Taber, Alberta" and my condition is recorded with the Japanese character for "good" (*yo-i*). The album says I was 19 1/2 inches. My birth weight was 7 lbs. 8 oz., and my blood type is B. My name is printed in Japanese, except for the "Sally" part. In full, it reads "Ito Sachiko Sally." I was given this name by my paternal grandmother.

Sachiko means "happy child." It is my Japanese name and not used by anyone except my mother, who always referred to me as "Sa-chan" when I was growing up. It is a common Japanese name, for who does not want their child to be happy? Sachiko was also my secret name, the name of my Japanese self, rarely used but secretly felt almost every day of my life. Chiyoko, my Japanese-Canadian grandmother, the woman who gave me this name, was also a woman who once said of her life, "*Un ga warui.* Fate is bad."

Born in Canada, but shuttled between Japan and Canada before and after the war against her will, first by her father and then her husband, Chiyoko had struggled all her life with an identity that was never her own. *Un ga warui.* Fate is bad. Like the subject-less language Japanese frequently appears to be, the direct English-to-Japanese transliteration implies a subject: the 'my' that should be in front of the word 'fate' or the 'to me' that should end the sentence. Except, in Japanese, all that is clear in the phrase is that 'fate' is the subject and that the object of that fate feels it is 'bad.' Here is an identity built in words, shaped by implication and absence. Had I not come to understand this language as my own— my literal mother tongue—my grandmother would have never been able to describe her life to me in this way.

Perhaps the act of naming me Happy Child in Japanese was one of hope against circumstance, a talisman to protect me from future harm. How I would grow into that secretively happy Japanese identity from the fate that made it so 'bad' for my family in the past is also, perhaps, the reason why I am writing this story.

"Sally," on the other hand, was a name suggested by my mother's younger sister, my aunt Michiko. At the time of my birth, she was a fifteen-year-old teenager attending a private Catholic girls' school in Osaka. Michiko was an avid reader. In a novel she was reading at the time, there was a female character of mixed race named "Sa-ri" or "Sally," as the English phonetic equivalent would be. The Chinese characters for the name, appended phonetically, stand for "gossamer village." The name had a foreign, exotic ring to it, unlike so many of the names ending with 'ko' that were given to girls in Japan.

For a long time, I thought my English name, Sally, was given to me out of a convention undertaken by many Japanese Canadians at the time, to name their children with English names. The North American name "Sally" means "princess." But my English name was itself an expression, paradoxically, of a Japanese girl's delight at the foreign and exotic, which is what a niece born in the wilds of Canada must have seemed like to her.

Already the threads of two languages, two cultures were being woven into the gossamer village of my identity.

In 2006, my seventy-one-year-old mother, Akiko, was out on the front lawn of her home in suburban Alberta, pulling dandelions. In Japan, where she was from, the dandelion is a lovely yellow flower, not a weed to be expunged; but here in suburban North America, it was considered a blight. She raised her head, looked around at all the weeds, and thought, "I can't do this anymore." Suddenly everything—the house and lawn around it—felt too big for my mother, too much to care for by herself.

The house on Manchester Drive was a split-level, two-storey suburban residence, covering 167 square metres in Sherwood Park, a community east of Edmonton. A huge oil refinery was located between the two cities with towers and tanks that emitted smoke and brimstone like an industrial Mordor, the wealth of which formed the basis of the economy in Alberta. The house was nondescript, like so many of its kind in Sherwood Park, but it possessed the characters of its owners, my mom and dad, for thirty-odd years of their lives. It was the home from which I graduated high school and made my way into the world, going first to Japan, then university. I returned to it for my father's funeral in 1990, before leaving once more when I got married and moved to Winnipeg. Twice a year, every summer and at Christmas, I returned to this house with my children. This house was, as the Japanese call such a residence, the *honke*, or main house, of our family clan.

It was not unreasonable for my mother to want to downsize; all of her three children were now grown, married, and had families of their own. The other families on the street that we had grown up with had long since departed.

Although I believed it was a good idea for Mom to sell the house, I found it hard to face the fact of the impending event. My siblings and I were going to lose the only house that had ever been our childhood home. It was packed full of the treasures and detritus of our lives, and sorting through it all to prepare the place for the realtor was daunting.

Back for a week from Manitoba on my summer holidays, I helped Mom with some of the work. For me, this mostly meant going into the basement crawl space where everything was kept. As I hunched over cartons, trunks, and shelves full of things accumulated over Mom's forty years of living in Canada, I came to understand what a lifetime's accumulation and possession of things signifies. What does one *do* during one's life? What are the items that mark those phases and passages of life?

Deep in the back of my mother's basement were trunks made of tempered blue metal plating with brass clasps and corner fixtures. They were perfect rectangles, deep and wide, full of treasure: the trousseau of a bride who had sailed the seas to her new home in a foreign land. Mom came to Canada in 1962 from Osaka, Japan, aboard a ship that first docked in Seattle. She had with her all the possessions a Japanese bride of her generation would need to set up house. They were all packed in steamship trunks that had an almost Victorian air to them. Such a display of baggage—the word itself a shopworn metaphor—was clearly an indication that this departure was permanent, the mark of the immigrant.

The trunks held items that were redolent of my mother, this creature out of whom I had emerged but who was, in many ways, a stranger to me, for she was *Japanese* and the things she brought with her were cultural signifiers. She was, moreover, a Japanese *wife*, and must somehow be the country's representation to her husband's family and colleagues.

In the trunks were kimonos and their accompanying parts; from the white *tabi* socks to the brocaded rope *obijimes* used to bind the long, rectangular expanse of *obi* that unfurled like a screen with its tracery of vines and leaves, its patterns and images derived from the natural world of flora and fauna. The ethereal moon-white undergarments were there, sometimes made of silk, sometimes of cotton—*nagajuban*, they are called—with their ties and stays. There was the *makura*—a bean-shaped pillow—to be slipped under the obi to give it fullness, and there was footwear, too—the *zori*, slightly elevated and tapered, made out of shiny vinyl. When I was a girl, I'd make furtive forays into the basement and open the kimono trunks so that I could dip my hands into their silken streams, touch the ropy shine of the cords, run my hands on the nubby texture of the raised threads on the obi. The kimono is a garment of rectangles—panels, as it were—and thus easy to fold into quarters. They were kept in paper folders with paper stays and laid gently on top of one another in the trunks. There was, always, the faint odour of mothballs.

The kimonos rarely came out; only occasionally did Mom wear them. She did not do Japanese dance or the tea ceremony, times when a kimono would have been appropriate. The only kimono I remember her wearing when I was a child was a white one with the landscape of a court garden on it; the obi was gold, black, and bright vermillion. She and the wife of one of my dad's colleagues once did a swap where the wife wore the kimono and my mother wore her Klondike Days outfit, which was a lurid red and black sleeveless gown with a plunging neckline, trimmed with black lace, with a red ostrich feather headpiece to match. The two wives in their swapped 'costumes' could not have presented a more startling contrast of cultures. The Klondike Days outfit was a costume, however, and the kimono—well, for an immigrant woman of my mother's generation in North America—it became a costume, too: a costume of both an assumed and projected identity. And it was also, more significantly to me, something else. It was also *art*. For who could not help but be attracted to its beauty? Buried in trunks in the basement, the kimonos were treasure. *My* mother's treasure.

There were other things, too, in that basement. There were kimono remnants, with which my mother used to make Japanese dolls. There was a box of stiff doll bodies—rectangular and white, stuffed with straw with wires inside. There were no heads, feet, or hands, because these appendages were attached later after the doll had been clothed in a kimono made from the remnants. I stumbled across a box full of doll heads once. They were individually wrapped in clear plastic and had different hairstyles pertaining to their station and period in life. Some had elaborate geisha coifs with glittery hairpieces and others had more subdued matronly styles. The faces were powdery white, the painted eyes, demure. The hands were kept separately in another box. Once the hands were attached, exquisitely shaped fingers of the doll could be manipulated to hold parasols or fans.

For Mom, doll making was a hobby. I don't know where she learned it, but it was a traditional craft using traditional materials. Little did I know then that it would become a dying craft; she herself stopped making them when I was still quite young. The dolls were omnipresent fixtures in the memories of my early childhood home in Edmonton and on my paternal great-aunt Kay's buffet table at her farm in Opal, Alberta. The dolls stood on jet-black, lacquered square platforms, and were kept in glass display cases. Most of the dolls my mother made were of women, but she had one of the grimacing and scary *shi-shi mai kabuki* actor, with flowing white hair and an exaggerated angry expression painted in red and black all over its face. Was this doll beautiful? No, it was frightening; a frighteningly good representation of an art form that recognized the fierce beauty of anger. The shi-shi mai was a lion dance meant to drive away evil spirits.

The ceramics in my mother's basement were also beautiful. Vases and *kenzans*—the prickly metal disk used for positioning flowers in the vases—were used for *ikebana* flower arrangement. Mom wasn't a practitioner of this art form, but the few vessels she had were outstanding. These ceramic vases were unlike the dainty frippery of English china, but had *aji*, or "taste," from which emanated the subtle glow of *wabi-sabi*, that distinctive Japanese aesthetic of the ephemeral and beautiful. They were restrained, refined, and simple pieces, elegant and elemental. She had one beautiful vase, aquamarine blue. It had a bowl-shaped cup that stood on three cylindrical legs. Inside the cup one would place the kenzan with a bit of water, and then the flowers would be arranged into it. My mother loved that vase. She agreed, albeit with justifiable trepidation, to lend it out for the Japanese Canadian Centennial celebrations in 1977 for an ikebana demonstration, at which event one of the legs broke.

That story has made that vase memorable. Its peculiar and austere shape now reminds me of a metaphor I was taught about the Anglican church. The Anglican faith was described to me as being like a stool with three legs. The faith was built on Scripture, Reason, and Tradition. To be of the faith meant reading the scripture, thinking about it, and enacting the age-old traditional rituals associated with the thinking and the reading of the text. Although this metaphor was meant for religious instruction, it seems to apply also to one's cultural identity, for is not one's identity built upon the same three things: the reading of the text, the thinking on the text, and the practice that has evolved out of a contemplation of the text?

Instead of the metaphor of the stool, however, I had my mother's vase with a broken leg. *This* was my cultural metaphor—a beautiful, empty vase—into which I must find and place the flower of words. The legs unite, not for a firm seat of belief, but rather to uphold an emptiness into which the beauty of the world might be received.

If anything is to be said of the craft of writing oneself, perhaps this metaphor is the one most appropriate for a Japanese-Canadian woman.

In the backyard of the house, there is a fire pit made out of concrete cinder blocks that Mom used to burn weeds and garbage. As we get deeper into the work of culling and sorting out stuff that belonged to my dad, John, who died sixteen years earlier, I think of burning the paper items like old files, magazines, and newspapers. It was summer and the evenings were long; a fire seemed like a good idea. Moreover, I like making fires. Burning stuff is a purification.

I haul out boxes of old files filled with stock reports, credit card statements, and expired policies and warranties. I dump these thick bunches of paper into the fire pit and surround them with balls of newspaper. The newspapers catch quickly and burn instantly, but once the flame reaches the clumped stacks of personal papers—those documents that attempt to mark time by debts incurred and paid off, documents of protection for items, of the performance of companies—it fizzles out. These documents are like bricks and need to be pried apart, so I rip and shred, poke and scatter them as best as I can before trying again to light them with a match. Soon they catch, and once the fire really begins to burn, I start thinking about the story I've been wanting to write all these years. The stories of my parents' and grandparents' lives.

The flames, fiery orange, rise into the air, the heat emanating from them in shimmery clouds. They take on an irridescent hue as the sun slowly sinks beneath the horizon. My gaze goes past the fire and into the dimmer recesses of the garden, which is enveloped by the murk of night. The backyard is big, sloping like a triangular piece of pie with its broad, crusted end at the top of the hill by the house, and its tip further down the yard out of sight. On the edges are two garden beds. In the one not far from the fire pit, I see the dark shadow of a lodgepole pine brought to the house by my father's friend, Seiji, from Valemount when my father died. Seiji and Dad went *matsutake* mushroom hunting together. The matsutake grows under the lodgepole pine in the mountains, come autumn. It's a beautiful white mushroom with a piney scent; its flavour is subtle but distinctive, and it is the one wild mushroom that the Japanese have been unable to cultivate like the shiitake. It was considered a delicacy by the Japanese, expensive and much sought-after. Dad coveted that mushroom. For many autumns, after that first year he found some with Seiji in Valemount, we went on expeditions into the mountains, looking for this truffle-like treasure.

Seiji brought that lodegpole pine in a black bucket all the way from Valemount where he lived; I remember him carrying it to the house when he came to the funeral. His face was sad, scrunched up, tearful.

The death was sudden. An abrupt departure. Like an axe to a tree.

Seiji was not the only one to memorialize Dad with a tree. An acquaintance of Dad's—a Jewish lawyer—had a tree planted in Dad's memory in a grove in Israel. They had met through Dad's community work in Edmonton. There was a commemorative certificate issued, which hung on the wall of our family room for years. I don't know all the details of my Dad's relationship to this man, but Dad did a lot of interpreting work—Japanese to English and English to Japanese—in Edmonton. It started back in his days as an exiled twelve-year-old Japanese-Canadian boy in Mie Prefecture who could speak English to the American soldiers who were around in the postwar Occupation days. As he made his way through middle school, he kept his English up and eventually knew it as well as his own language, unlike his brothers, who would soon lose these abilities. He worked for the Occupation Forces as an interpreter just before he returned to Canada to begin his adult life here; he knew opportunities were better than what he could see in a dismal, exhausted country defeated by its enemies.

In Alberta, there were many exchanges between the provincial government and Japan. There were twinning arrangements between towns, cities, and even the province itself with other similar places in Japan, the hosting of a winter Olympics in Calgary, the building of a private Japanese high school campus in Spruce Grove—all of which required the services of a qualified interpreter. There were photographs of Dad with the Japanese speed skating team, and of him with the principal of the Japanese high school whose students we hosted or helped find hosts for. Dad had taken an early retirement from his federal government position as a radio operator and readily took on these jobs. During one of these stints, he interpreted once for former Prime Minister Joe Clark. For a long time, a framed photo of the two of them sat on our piano.

Dad's ability in the two languages was amazing, unsurpassed by anyone else in the community. He could listen to a speech given in English and, without taking notes, seamlessly interpret it into Japanese. A friend of the family, a Japanese scientist, said that Dad was the only one he knew who was able to do this kind of interpreting at such a high level of competency. There had apparently been some kind of contest in Edmonton, and Dad was the only one left at the end who could interpret the most complex of speeches.

I saw a picture of my father taken before he died, shown to me by a Japanese couple who had visited Alberta. I was in Japan on a Mombusho graduate scholarship the year before my father died, and was with a group of foreign students who had been sponsored on a trip to the Noto peninsula in Ishikawa Prefecture. The family

I stayed with—an old and venerable family of the area, judging by their large traditional house made of timbered wood—had visited Alberta and had had my father as a tour guide. They showed me pictures of him, and remarked upon his truly excellent Japanese.

As the evening descends and the firelight flickers and grows dimmer, I look at the shadow of the lodgepole, at the same time thinking of the tree—was it an olive?—in Israel. In my mind's eye, the two merge into one.

Next to the pit is a stack of cancelled cheques. I dump them into the fire. They land—*foof!*—on top of a pile of grey ash. I scatter them with my poker. On each of the cheques is my father's signature, so stylized it is illegible as actual letters. It is a flourished cipher, repeated over and over again, a combination of "K J I," standing for Kunitaro John Ito. Now these signatures are floating their way into another world; it's as if I am returning them to the hand that once wrote them. But as I watch the paper burn, I think, too, that however much I thought I knew Dad, he was more like his signature in my life, a stylized, Romanized cipher of his name. Robustly confident, but ultimately illegible.

Later, in a box in a basement, I find Dad's old diary from when he returned to southern Alberta as a young man to where his grandparents, Saichi and Ei, and his Uncle Jack and Aunt Molly were living after the war. It's a tan, faux-leather bound book with "One Year Diary" embossed in gold print on the front and with a gold clasp on the side with a keyhole. Luckily, the clasp opens without a key. In the front, there is an identification section, which my dad has filled in with salient but cursory details: Name: *John Kunitaro Ito.* My Weight Is: *130 lbs.* Height: *5' 1".* Color of Hair: *Black.* Color of Eyes: *Brown.* He did not fill in the address section, or any of the records section in which you were to fill in your Automobile License No., Car and Motor No., and the location of your Valuable Papers. This was probably because he had no vehicle to speak of, and no location for his valuable papers, living as he was at his uncle's house. But in Sizes to Remember, he wrote a '6' for Shoes. The opening pages of the diary contain, among other things, Your Horoscope and What Did the Stars Foretell at Your Birth. I look at the entry for my father's birthdate, February 22 (Pisces), and it reads: *Natural wanderers. Lack concentration and directness. Adaptability to circumstances and environment may be their salvation. Careless with money. Genial and life of party. Essentially lazy; most domestic. Sub-conscious mind is better mind. Makes a good friend.*

The diary entries bear no actual calendar year, but Dad sometimes put the day of the week on the entry, so from that I calculated the year to have been 1957. The entries exist only from January 22 to April 2, the crucial months in which my father began to forge his destiny in Canada. Most of the entries are written in English, but occasionally Japanese *kanji* characters appear here and there. As I flip through the pages, a slip of paper falls out. It contains several doodle-like inscriptions in my father's hand. I look more closely. Why, he's practising his signature! That now-recognizable flourish was on all those cancelled cheques I had just burnt in the fire.

This was the first entry in the diary: *Worked for Nagai Bros. from 8 a.m. to 10 p.m. washing turnips (15 tons) at Plunkett & Savage. Had supper at Coaldale café and trimmed turnips for 12 ton order to be washed tomorrow until 10:00 p.m. Am very tired cause of constant scaling and loading. Specially my legs. Received check from Bill Nagai for work from Dec. 22 to Jan. 19. Decided today to write my diary daily. Should have started it long time ago.*

From then on, there are daily entries until April 2. His fluid handwriting is assured, smooth, and readable, and he is direct about his feelings—*Generally speaking, I felt lousy today*—and yet, at the same time, he expresses constant frustration with himself and his shortcomings—*Should study but am tired. Always making excuses.*

Dad was at a juncture in his life at which he had to choose a vocation—*Should I see a psychologist and have him analyse myself as to what kind of job I should take up?*—while also feeling the burden of responsibility as the oldest son to make good on his decision to return to Canada and help his remaining brothers back in Japan—*last night wrote letters to Shiro about procedures concerning gratification of Canadian citizenship.* Education, he knew, was the road to self-improvement and better opportunities, but he also knew time was short if he wanted to be in the best position to sponsor the rest of his family back to Canada.

During these dark winter months, where he sometimes laboured for long hours, trimming turnips and cabbages for the local farm businesses in the area, he also took correspondence courses like Essential Math and a diesel engine course, ordered records from Columbia Record Club—*Got my third and last free record from C.R. Club, a selection of Jerome Kern's music conducted by Andre Kostelanetz. Not so hot*—observed with acuity the difficult domestic relationship between his Aunt Molly and his grandmother—*Auntie's eyes were bloodshot. Grandma must have caused trouble again, making her weep*—and described the conditions of a prairie winter—*When I woke up, I was surprised to discover that a warm chinook was blowing. It melted the snow quite a lot so now could see mostly bare ground. Started to freeze again after dark, though.* It was during this period he also saw his first hockey game—*Went with Bobby to civic center to watch my first hockey game. It was played between Lethbridge and Medicine Hat team. Medicine Hat team won 8–1.*

There were a few occasions when Dad wrote in Japanese, usually words or phrases having to do with the Buddhist church or special terms like "*Sensei*," but I did find it curious when, at one point, he switched into Japanese script to express a fear that the local post office might be keeping mail from him. From what I could tell from his diary entries, Dad was receiving a lot of mail from Japan then: letters from friends, and, notably, magazines. So, during the winter months, he was obviously reading a lot, too, and not just in English but in Japanese. He doesn't mention the Japanese material much, probably because it would have been a bother to translate the titles, but he does mention the reading he does in English, which, it seems, he did more out of study than for entertainment: *Read a couple of articles in the Saturday Evening Post (old edition) and looked up unknown words in the dictionary and wrote them down in my two-ring binder.*

In one entry, he writes of being asked to interpret for an elderly couple wanting to become naturalized citizens: *Today I was asked by Michiko to interpret [for] her mother and father-in-law when they went to the courthouse at 2:00 p.m. to apply for naturalization. I went with them and the difficult part of it was that I had to interpret an oath in Buddhism.*

I'm not sure how conscious Dad was of his Japaneseness in the context of his new, ostensibly multicultural country, but there were a few mentions of other minorities living in the area. In one entry, he writes: *Seems like the Indians working for the Nagai's have their domestic troubles, too. Robert and Wilfred was complaining that John Bottle is living with them, making it cramped and that he's using their coal for fuel.* And when he went for a job in Lethbridge on the recommendation of a friend, he writes: *I went to Nakamuras first, and then I went to see the Chinaman. He told me to come to work on the 16th.* "Chinaman," "Indian"—those were the English words of the day used to describe Chinese Canadians and Indigenous peoples, but I wonder if Dad ever thought of himself as a "Jap" in this context. And nowhere is the mention of the word "white."

In the four months of entries in this journal, Dad grapples with what he should do with his life. He is at a crossroads and, moreover, feels uncomfortable living with his uncle and aunt and their brood of children, who, in the traditional manner, are also looking after his aged grandfather, Saichi, and grandmother, Ei. As a young, single man recently arrived in the country, at loose ends with himself, he finds that he is out of step with the others. On February 10, he writes: *Really got bawled out from grandma today. She blamed me for her and the rest of the family not getting along so well. This made me pretty mad although there is one thing I must admit*

... I've treated her badly and my attitude to her is of a scornful kind. I've been avoiding her and rejecting her advice and her kindness. I try to reason this by the fact that this attitude of mine towards her developed after I noticed the trouble [between her and Molly] *but I still feel bad about it.*

Dad then contemplates going to the coast: *Am considering leaving and heading for Vancouver this spring. Jack Nagai has kindly suggested that he'll write a letter of recommendation to a vegetable wholesaler if I want a job at his place in Vancouver.* Later he writes: *Talked with Kuma. He says I should go east to Toronto instead of going to Vancouver. It might be a good idea to write to the Japanese Canadian newspaper there and also write to the people I know there.*

In the meantime, he goes to Lethbridge to look for employment at the National Employment Service office there with the intent of moving off the farm and into the city in the spring. Afterwards, he checks out a lead at a shoe store and then heads to the Air Force recruiting office to get information: *Joining the RCAF is sure attractive to me.* On his return to the farm, he records: *It's kinda hard to break out what I want to do with uncle and aunt.* On the following day: *I'm in a turmoil on whether I should join up with the RCAF or take a job in Lethbridge. Maybe I should go and see a psychiatrist and take an aptitude test to see what I really want to do. Sure am mixed up.*

Grand dream vs. hard reality. I'm not sure how my 5' 1", 130 lbs. father with glasses, who was an obsessive reader in two languages, would have fared in the air force if he had joined, but it seems my uncle and aunt had a sobering chat with him about his dreams: *Tonite, I talked it over with aunt and uncle after they returned from Lethbridge. Toronto yuki, Vancouver iki and the RCAF was abandoned, and as the prospects of working in a grocery store was better than in a shoe store, it was decided that I would go and see this Chinese grocery store owner whom May Nakamura recommended me.*

Dad eventually moves out to Lethbridge, where he takes a room, starts working at the grocery store, and begins his life as an independent adult in Canada. His last entry on April 2 is brief: *Rented couple of records at library. Also borrowed a book to read.*

That fall, he would go to Calgary to enroll in the Radio and Electronics Program at the Provincial Institute of Technology and Art in their Commercial Wireless Operating Course. He appears in the 1957–58 yearbook as a young man with a round face, glasses, and black hair slicked back, wearing a suit with broad lapels and a bright tie with a splotched print design.

As was fitting with his natural abilities in communication, Dad would become a radio operator.

At the end of the week, the garage was filled with contents of the basement arranged on long tables. We planned a garage sale that my sister and sister-in-law offered to manage. I took away a few choice items but there is little I can haul in a van already filled with children and holiday luggage.

The night before, I sat on the steps of the basement and cried. *How could this be happening,* I thought, *with no one to tell the story of this family, this house's inhabitants?* And a deeper, darker part of me also thought, *Who cares?*

In the upcoming year, my husband was going to be on sabbatical from his teaching position at his university. We were going to go to Japan, where I hoped to investigate the family history for a book and to let our children experience life in Japan. I'd applied for a grant and was crossing my fingers that the money would come through for us to make this trip possible.

My mother knew our plans and was in favour of them. A few years previous, she had given me her father's memoir. He titled it *Rorai no Ki* ("A Record of Remembrance from Old Age") and intended to leave the document as a legacy for his children and grandchildren. The memoir was a printed document, typed up on a *wa-pro,* the Japanese name for a "word processor," which my urbane and cultivated grandfather, Toshiro Saito, had taken to like the proverbial duck to water to record his memoir in 1989. I had known of this memoir's existence for years and its home in my mother's dresser. But as interested as I was, I couldn't read it. It was like those volumes of Tolstoy and Balzac that Mom had brought with her from Japan along with her art postcards of Monet and Degas. These things, too, while being a presence in the house, I had rediscovered in my mother's basement. The books were elegant, hardback editions of Western classics in Japanese text. Inside one was the famous Delacroix painting of Chopin, his ivory-coloured face tilted, looking wistfully upwards. These European romantic paintings reminded me that Mom had been a painter herself; there was an oil painting of hers in the house—a still life array with a plant, bottles, and an open book—that she had exhibited once in Osaka.

I knew my grandfather's memoir contained a world of culture that I had gotten a whiff of in my cursory inspection of my mother's books and postcards. But I had no access to it. It was an impenetrable, walled-garden of a text I longed to get into but couldn't.

Misuzu Kaneko, the Japanese children's poet whom I have been translating, has a wonderful poem about books. Her parents ran a bookstore in Senzaki during the early Showa period in Japan that might have sold fashionable, elegant editions of European classics in their original languages, like the translated ones my mother had on her shelf. Misuzu, however, did not know her father; he died when she was two, and all she had of him were stories that her mother must have told of him. And his *books*.

The Book

When I'm lonely, I go to my absent father's room
and stare at the gold print on the bindings
of the books on the shelf.

Sometimes I stand on my tippy toes and stealthily reach
for a heavy book that I pull out and wrap in my arms like a doll.

I take it to the bright verandah.

Inside the book, it's all horizontal writing
without any kana at all; but the pattern of it looks beautiful
and it has a strange scent

Licking my finger, I turn white page after page,
making up story after story in there.
In the verandah in May
where the sun streams in
making shadows of fresh leaves
flutter on the letters,
how truly I love to read that great big book.

—Misuzu Kaneko

Words in books are the foundation of any literate culture, and
its subsequent reading practice is what forms the culture of the
reader. For me, however, Japanese words were something I could
never actually *read* very well, but, like Misuzu, I could at least perceive that such books were beautiful containers of culture, and,
lo, like Misuzu, I could fill them with imagined stories. And such
stories could evoke the memory of people who were absent, people
who were a mystery, and whom we longed to love.

Toshiro Saito, my maternal grandfather, was that mystery of a person in a text. But in order for me to access that mystery, I would need help with its translation, and the only person who could help me was my mother's sister, Michiko, in Japan. Although my mother helped me with translation on the occasions we would visit together, Michiko, who had gone to university for a year in Alberta and studied literature, could give me the sustained time and energy required for translating a document of this size and scope. She was already looking to find a place for us to live in Japan and knew I was coming to enlist her help in translating her father's words into English.

But there was another absence, too—my paternal grandmother, Chiyoko's—which I also longed to investigate. Her absence was the result of the Pacific War and the actions taken against Japanese Canadians during that time. It is through her line that I am a Canadian; it is through her line that our family can trace its generations of connections to Japan.

Chiyoko, however, never wrote a book. I would not find her story in a text; instead, I heard it, or bits of it, either in Japanese or the mix of Japanese and English spoken by her sister, my Auntie Kay, who lived in Alberta. Born in Canada, but shuttled between Japan and Canada before and after the war, Chiyoko had struggled all her life with an identity that was never her own.

The Ito story, therefore, was oral, delivered to me in childhood by the one who was present, my grandmother's sister, my Auntie Kay. Kay and Chiyoko's father, Saichi, was first to come to Canada at the turn of the century, and everything I knew about him came from Auntie Kay. Saichi and Ei, his wife, did live long enough to at least hold my infant body in their arms in 1964. There is a photo testifying to this event. The Itos are seated in a cluttered living room in a farmhouse, probably the one belonging to Saichi and Ei in Cranford, Alberta, not far from the hospital where I was born in Taber.

After that, my gaze on the ancestors who had come over a century ago from Japan would only ever fall on a black and white photo of them—an elderly couple: Saichi with a long, angular face with high cheekbones and sunken cheeks, in a suit; Ei beside him, shorter, with a round face and tiny eyes, the left one almost closed shut, with a black pillbox planted on her head, wisps of netting floating above the hat. This photo dwelled in Auntie Kay's *butsudan*, Buddhist altar, in the farmhouse she lived in with her husband, Sanjiro, in Opal. The butsudan was a big black box, everything in it dark and smoky, except for the dim radiance emanating from the image of the Buddha. The butsudan was an important place; it was where you put pictures of the dead and remembered them. You'd light a stick of incense, ring the resonant, bowl-shaped bell with a mallet, put your hands together, bow, and pray, which is what Auntie Kay would do from time to time. Pray to the ancestors, pray to her parents, for they were *her* parents—Saichi and Ei—they were the ones who had brought her into this world, into Canada, on the banks of the Fraser River where it met the Pacific Ocean; a fertile, teeming place of salmon and sealife, lined with docks, fishing boats, and canneries.

According to Auntie Kay— and from what I would later corroborate from documents, namely, the Ito *koseki-tohon*, or Ito family registry—Saichi was recorded as being from Sobue, Nakashima-gun, in Aichi Prefecture in Japan when he had left the country for North America. In sociological terms, Saichi was the first-generation, classic Type A personality risk-taker. He was a pioneer. A true Issei.

According to the registry, Saichi was born in 1875, and was the *chonan*, the eldest son, of rural landowner Kiyozaemon and his wife, Kyau. Saichi's birth came a few years after the Meiji Restoration when the emperor of Japan was restored to the throne and Japan began its rapid ascent into modernity. The times were tumultuous but exciting. *Risshin Shusse*, or "Getting on in the World," was a catchphrase of the day, and many people aspired to raise themselves above their common lot in society. The Meiji period was also when large-scale emigration began. People migrated first out of the villages into the cities, and then further afield to countries such as Canada, the United States, and Brazil.

Improving his lot in life, however, was not the reason Saichi left Japan. Family lore had it that Saichi was a gambler. Having racked up debts with the local *yakuza* gangsters in his obsession with the beguiling card game of *hanafuda*—played with small black cards decorated with seasonal floral motifs such as the cherry blossom and the wisteria—he clearly needed an avenue of escape. Word had it that someone in the neighbouring village had gone to Canada. The seed of this idea planted in his head, Saichi ran off to the port of Yokohama, leaving his parents with the shameful stigma of his departure, an act considered unfilial and irresponsible. Thus began the "Ito jinx"—the departure of the eldest son in a pattern that would continue for generations right up through to my father and even into my cousin's line. Sixteen-year-old Saichi would be a stowaway on one of the steamships that plied the Pacific during those years and, after a short spell earning his keep as a cabin boy on one of these ships, he finally set foot in Victoria, British Columbia, in early 1890.

Like other young Japanese men who arrived on Canada's west coast at that time, Saichi probably had no intention of staying. He would work off his gambling debts, see a bit of the new country, and eventually return home to restore the family name and take his rightful place as heir. But things would take much longer than expected, and, furthermore, Saichi fell into a line of work that strangely suited his old penchant for gambling: fishing. The Fraser River teemed with salmon, ripe for harvesting. Already in Steveston, highly skilled fishermen who'd come from Japan's coastal Prefectures were doing well. Saichi joined them. However, Saichi was an atypical fisherman. Ever the feckless gambler, he'd venture out into stormy weather, lashing himself to his boat with a rope in case he was tossed overboard, and fish until his boat heaved with his catch. He cared not a whit for his boat or his safety. The others were too attached to their vessels, he felt; for him, the boat was merely a means to an end. Fishing to the extreme meant that he could purchase a new boat engine every year, and with it (and the protection of the gods, procured with a generous donation to the Buddhist temple) Saichi would set out to sea and fish with relish.

By 1907, Saichi was a prosperous young man with a stable occupation. It was time to marry. Unlike some of his peers who had to make do with picture brides, Saichi could afford to go home to Sobue to marry the woman his family had chosen for him. He would wed his cousin, Ei, from nearby Gifu Prefecture. The main house, or honke, taken over by Saichi's younger brother, Sentaro, now looked on Saichi with reverence and respect. The wayward prodigal had returned not only completely reformed but rich, to boot. And as there was yet more money to be made in the new country, Saichi was intent on going back. He and Ei would start their own dynasty of Japanese Canadians in British Columbia. The following year, in 1908, their first child, my grandmother, Chiyoko, was born. Soon after that, Koji 'Jack' was born, followed by Kiyoe 'Kay' in 1914.

Growing up in Sherwood Park for most of my childhood, I visited Auntie Kay's farm frequently, especially during spring and summer. Her little wooden farmhouse, which she and her husband, Sanjiro, built together in the 1950s, remains in my memory like a chapel in the woods one stumbles on in dreams. At night, when I swim in the under-waters of my consciousness, the house and the farm often appear: the mystical woods with their poplar and spruce trees, the saskatoons and pin cherries hanging like jewels off the long limbs of their willowy, nymph-like bodies, the beds of moss and dank grass from out of which emerged spongy mushrooms and cream-white puffballs. In front of the house was a vast strawberry patch, a remnant of the farming life Kay had before in Surrey with her parents and her sister's and brother's families. On the side of the house was a large asparagus patch, which we picked from every spring for decades. The front of the house had two entrances. One had concrete steps, at the bottom of which were planted peonies that bloomed fistfuls of white, pink, and burgundy flowers every June. It was on these steps that dozens of family photos were taken, generations squatting, sitting, or standing by the tiered entryway with baskets, bags, and boxfuls of fruits and vegetables gleaned from the garden. At the top of the stairs was a screened doorway to a tiny vestibule that led into the living room. Once, when I was in Grade 2 and we were staying in the farmhouse for the summer while Auntie Kay and Sanjiro visited Japan, I witnessed a thunder and lightning storm from that screen window. It was a storm of spectacular beauty—the kind that would make the poet Shelley run naked into it—with pealing claps of thunder and sizzling bolts of lightning. The thunderclap was the signal for the curtain of darkness to be lifted, when suddenly one could catch sight of the rows of strawberry plants, the apple trees that bordered them, the rickety outbuildings and green-roofed garage, beyond which was a vast field of grain and the gravel road to the far left, where there might appear a dark vehicle heading towards the highway in the distance.

It was on top of those stairs that my aunt would yell for her husband when the evening meal was ready. "Sanjiro!" she would call him, using his proper first name for years like any English-speaking Canadian would for their husband or wife. It wasn't until she went to Japan with him on that trip in the 1970s that she was told by her in-laws to refer to her husband as "Sanjiro-*san*," for it was important for the wife to add the honorific 'san' to the name as a sign of respect. Meanwhile, of course, Sanjiro continued calling Kay by her Japanese name "Kiyoe" without the 'san', to no chastisement. We children called him *Jiji*, a derogatory Japanese word, in fact, meaning the equivalent of "dirty old man" (sad to say, a name only too true). Sanjiro was irascible and lecherous—he'd try to slap or squeeze my mother's or my other aunts' buttocks, and he had a temper, to boot; I don't know how my great-aunt put up with him. I would discover later that he was fond of her, although

I was never really quite sure how much she loved him. He was her second husband; her first had died young of a heart attack in the years just after the war when they had left the internment centre in Popoff to go to the Okanagan.

The other entrance to the house was at ground level. A cement pad had been laid in front of the wooden door and it was edged by empty plant pots and containers used for harvesting vegetables. A rain barrel stood nearby. That barrel was a source of fascination for me. One afternoon, when my siblings and I collected frogs from a nearby holding pond, I got the idea of putting them into the rain barrel. Once the small, quivering frogs were deposited they would set out, star-shaped, stretching their bodies into the inky darkness of the water, in a way that reminded me of shooting stars in the cosmos; thus was the eponymous poem of my first book of poetry, *Frogs in the Rain Barrel*, borne from that childhood experience.

The ground-level entrance and its stairwell leading to the kitchen is where Auntie Kay resides in memory and in metaphor. The working entrance to the house, it had a large, closed-in, dirt-floored room filled with planters, baskets, and garden tools. In my earliest memory of that room, there was also a wringer washer there and a large freezer. Everything was grimy and gritty with that farmhouse functionality that understands dirt to be its fundamental element. It was in here that vegetables were sorted and washed, that seeds, tubers, and bulbs were kept. Farm tools hung from hooks with twine on the walls. There were flies. Lots of them, buzzing around the room, rattling at the windowsills. Sometimes there would be long strips of fly paper hanging from the ceiling. If I picture anyone in this room at all, it is Auntie Kay, hunched over, tending to something: a bucket, a basket, or pail. She had sloped shoulders, which I seem to have inherited, much to my mother's chagrin, but instead of hovering over the desk, toiling at a screen full of words, she paid her attention to the ground and the fruits thereof; she was a farmer through and through.

And a storyteller. Practically everything I know about the Ito family history came through her. She was the lore keeper—not in any deliberate way, for she was not a teacher or a scribe like my urbane maternal grandfather in Osaka, but a childless woman who doted on her grand-niece and fed her appetite for stories with ones from her past.

She told me of what it was like growing up on the docks of a cannery on the mouth of the Fraser River, a dangerously precarious place for children: "Oh, Mama was afraid we'd fall into the water, running around like that," she had said. And you could see from the old pictures, in those stilts and pilings that supported the wooden docks, how right her mother was, and how difficult it would have been to prevent the children from running or lying down on the rough-hewn planks to peer into the salty waters below and watch the waves wash and foam at the edges of the pillars that descended into the depths of the sea.

I felt that way when, as a child, I peered down the old well by the pig barn at the farm, giddy on the threshold, both curious and frightened by the dark, dank wetness below into which the bucket plunged, splashed, and brought up the silvery reflections of our faces. I was warned to stay away from the well; it was not safe for children, obviously. I knew the well was there for getting water for the pigs' troughs. Auntie Kay and Sanjiro had raised various livestock over the years—turkeys, chickens, pigs.

Auntie Kay was with me at the well and dropped the bucket until I heard it splash, then retrieved it by yanking up the length of the rope, hand over hand. I see her now looming in front of me—a solid woman of firm, fit flesh—bringing up a bucket of water from the well, proficient with a gracefulness that was hers alone. Those arms and hands hoed, shovelled, pulled weeds, planted seeds, rooted through forest floors for mushrooms, picked and plucked berries both wild and domestic, and even wielded a rifle on occasion when necessary to clear the area of coyotes. Clearly, she was a woman of the land.

But in the beginning, this hardy prairie farmer had been a fisherman's daughter who lived by the sea. And if it hadn't been for the war, she probably would have stayed on that coast—the sea an ever present entity, never far away and always beckoning—and would have become ... what? A strawberry farmer, probably, for that is what she and her first husband were doing when they were so abruptly forced to leave.

By the time I knew Auntie Kay and put my childish hand into hers on the farm as we walked to the well together, she and Sanjiro had already been in Alberta for over twenty-five years. A bucolic pace of life had been established, a complacency of domesticity into which our family's common day lives were interwoven as seamlessly as they had been before the war when my father had been a child and wandered over to his auntie's house for a treat those long-ago years in Surrey.

The tragedy, and perhaps the back-handed blessing of Providence, was that Auntie Kay effectively became our Canadian grandmother, a close enough relative with a farm and with whom to share Christmases and summers. She was among those who stayed and persevered to make a go out of a country that did not want them.

When, as a girl and then later as an adult, I was curious and asked Auntie Kay for stories, it was like asking her to lower the bucket into the well. She would do it willingly for me, dipping that bucket into those murky, painful depths, extracting stories to meet my thirst, and for this I will always be grateful.

The stories burbled in my head for years. Always I meant to write them; always they were a book in my mind. But it had been a long time since I'd asked Auntie Kay for stories, and after I moved to Winnipeg in 2000, I saw her infrequently. She was in a care home in Calgary then, looked in on by my aunt and uncle who lived there. As my mother caught me up on family news and my plans for travel to Japan in 2007, she casually asked, "Do you know there is land left in Saichi's name in Japan?"

What? Auntie Kay had never mentioned anything about this to me. Of course, she told me how her father had been dispossessed of his farmland in Surrey during the war and then relocated to the sugar beet fields of Alberta. He was elderly by then, but, ever the patriarch, told Kay, who was childless, to stay behind in Surrey with her sister, Chiyoko, to mind the five children while their husbands were taken off to road camp in the Rockies. The two sisters with the five children ended up at Hastings Park, the field and livestock grounds of the Pacific National Exhibition in Vancouver, before being shipped off to Lemon Creek, in the Slocan Valley region of southeastern British Columbia.

My curiosity was piqued. Since I was going to Japan, I could investigate this old land claim. Would it be possible that I or any of Saichi's descendants in Canada might inherit his land in Japan? This was a completely crazy idea, a pipe dream of the worst kind, but there it was. I wondered what the land looked like. It would probably be near Sobue where Saichi came from. Sobue, which had formerly been part of Nakashima County, had been subsumed into the municipality of Inazawa, just outside of the city of Nagoya in Aichi Prefecture. How far outside, I wondered. Was there a house on the place? If there was, what condition was it in?

The least I could do on this trip was find out something about the mystery of this land—where it was, what it looked like, and who lived on it—for it was from there, over a hundred years ago, that Saichi had set out to come to Canada.

Chapter Two:

Beautiful North

It is north too but it is Beautiful

—Sally Ito, 7 years old.

Before we moved permanently to the house in Sherwood Park, my family lived for a time in the Northwest Territories. Dad's early career as a radio operator with the federal government's Department of Transport began in the far north, in Sachs Harbor. After Mom and Dad were married, he was posted to Fort Wrigley on the banks of the Mackenzie River. They returned to Edmonton for a spell, until Dad got transferred to Hay River. I was seven at the time, about to enter Grade 2, and we were going to drive up to Hay River in the summer of 1972. In excited anticipation of the move, I drew a picture in blue crayon of a snow-capped mountain that looked like Mount Fuji. Above it, I wrote: *The Eskmos Live in the Noth where the ice and snow, but on our hloday it is noth too but it is Beautiful.*

After packing up our things in a huge Allied moving van, our family made the long drive up from Edmonton on the only road that extends into the Northwest Territories from Alberta: the Mackenzie Highway. At some point, this highway turned into a gravel road, a clear sign we were departing from the civilized world of the city into the wilderness. For my mother, this was her second foray into the North. When she'd married Dad in 1962, their first residence had been in Fort Wrigley. At that time, Fort Wrigley was nothing but a small compound of five houses belonging to government employees. Dad worked in a little radio hut a stone's throw away from the house. Food, most of it canned, including evaporated milk and also butter, was flown in by helicopter. For Mom, a former resident of Osaka, the second-most populous city in Japan, the contrast was startling and, at times, unbearable. For almost two years, she struggled to get pregnant, and suffered through stifling isolation in a house smothered in darkness for several months.

The house, a quaint two-storey building of white clapboard with red trim, was located close to the Mackenzie River. For a good part of the year, the river was frozen; a vast, impenetrable plain of ice and snow. Mom must have looked out at the river several times a day like a confined animal in its cage. For months on end, the view was the same. With her husband away in the radio hut, she would make her Japanese dolls, sew or embroider, and sometimes she painted or drew. I found watercolour paintings of the house in an unfinished sketchbook in the basement, a testament to her 'idle' pursuits of the time.

When spring arrived, it was announced by the raucous break-up of the river, the ice cleaving into chunks and jagged slabs that carved and ground against the bank. My mother spoke of this with awe and wonderment, as if the river had read her mind, her captive and soporific state, breaking up, released at last.

Now we were on that same namesake highway, the Mackenzie, trundling northwards again, and if my mother had any trepidation about this move, I couldn't tell. Things were vastly different for her this time: she was now a mother of three, two of whom were toddlers. And Hay River was an actual town, not a government settlement like Fort Wrigley.

We stopped at the border, which was marked by a large billboard featuring the logo of the Territories, a polar bear surrounded by blue. Scrambling out of the car, I clambered up onto the concrete platform on which the billboard stood, the family following me, where we posed for a photo. In the broad sunlight, I stood off by myself, while my sister and brother, barely a year apart, were held by my parents.

Like any child, my head was filled with ideas about what my new life in the North would be like. My childish writing expresses the stereotypical—Eskimos, ice, and snow—but how, I wonder, did I at that age know how to spell the word "beautiful"?

Once we crossed into the Northwest Territories, we stopped at our first sightseeing spot: Alexandra Falls. The falls are the third largest in the Territories and a spectacular display of thundering brown water falling over a precipice of thirty-two metres. There were no fences or barriers at the falls; you could walk right to its edge on a slab of stone and feel the spray and hear the juddering sound of the river leaping into the frothy abyss below. In Japan, Canada was advertised by tourist agencies as "Big Nature." *Dai Shizen.* My experience of Dai Shizen was standing on the edge of those falls. They were bigger than anything I could ask for or imagine.

Hay River was located on the south shore of Great Slave Lake. It was divided into two sections: Old Town and New Town. Between the two and slightly westward was the airport where my father worked. Our house was in New Town in a newly created subdivision. It was a spacious brown bungalow built into a shallow cul-de-sac with other similar houses nearby. My mother decorated the house with her usual Japanese things, including a big gold *byobu*, or folding screen panel, of a flowering tree that she put above the couch and that would be a mainstay of our living room décor for years. We had no TV reception in the house, except after seven o'clock, but that changed with the advent of the Anik telecommunications satellite the following year.

As a federal government employee, my father was of the

suburban white-collar class, and many of his fellow government workers lived with their families in the same neighbourhood. I played with their children. There were no other Asians in New Town, except the Chows—Flora and Bob—who did not have any children. Mom and Dad occasionally played mah-jong with them. Bob worked with Dad at the airport. Not long after we arrived in town, Dad found out about a Japanese woman—Kathy was her English name—married to an Iranian named Rashid. Mom and Kathy quickly made friends, especially as her two children were the same age as my younger brother and sister.

New Town was not far from the centre of Hay River, which was within walking distance and had all the major facilities: post office, swimming pool, skating rink, stores, the high school and an elementary school for the upper grades, a hospital, library, and some churches. My life revolved mostly around New Town. Although the lake was a massive geographical entity, I don't recall seeing it much except for the odd shoreline glimpse on our occasional drives into Old Town. The Hay River, though, flowed not far behind the houses of my neighbourhood and I recall scrambling along its muddy banks in early summer.

For school, I was to start Grade 2 in Old Town which was on the other end of Hay River, a drive rather than a walk away, through New Town, over the river, and past the airport. Old Town was *older*; the elementary school looms in memory as a wooden behemoth that felt ancient compared with the suburban elementary school I had gone to in Edmonton. There was a primitive mission-school quality to that place, as if it were perched on the edge of the frontier. The school-yard was muddy and had old playground equipment. There was a large, towering set of wooden swings that looked almost like a gallows with worn planks for swing seats and thick iron chain links that were attached to a broad iron beam far above.

The Grade 2 teacher was Miss Kurchaba. A tall, ethereal woman in my memory, the only picture that comes to mind was of her head, covered in soft blonde curls, wrapped in a see-through chiffon kerchief when she went out. My love of reading began in her class. I started the year with *Clifford the Big Red Dog* books, but by the end of that year those books seemed simple; by then, I had moved on to attempting to read *The Secret Garden* by Frances Hodgson Burnett.

My mother read vicariously with me. In my picture books of the time, I would find *hiragana* or kanji characters scribbled in the margins or above the English words, giving the word's definition in Japanese. We went occasionally to the public library, which was not a far walk from where we lived. Not long after our arrival, the Hay River Public Library had a drawing contest for kids on their favourite books. I submitted a drawing of a favourite character of mine from a book I loved: *Anatole and the Piano* by Eve Titus, illustrated by Paul Galdone. Anatole was a French mouse who lived on the outskirts of Paris and had adventures described in a series of *Anatole* books. I loved drawing the triangular-faced mouse with his big black eyes, jaunty beret, and bright red scarf. My picture won. The prize for the contest was Ronald Melzack's *The Day Tuk Became a Hunter,* which became my introduction to the mythological world of the Inuit. Winning that prize whetted my appetite for contests, and I would continue submitting to them in the future.

Apart from my increasing interest in reading, the most memorable part of Grade 2 was my learning about Japan. Unbeknownst to me, my father had gone ahead to the school and talked with them about my unusual situation as the only child in the classroom to belong to a visible minority. Was it his suggestion or the teacher's that the class do a unit on Japan? Dad was not an educator, but as far as he was concerned, his children would *own* their identities by becoming informed about them at the earliest possible age.

From this unit in Grade 2, I learned the basic facts about Japan. There were four main islands in the country: Hokkaido, Honshu, Kyushu, and Shikoku. The capital was Tokyo. There was an emperor who ruled the nation. Japan was volcanic, and on the Pacific Ring of Fire, so there were earthquakes from time to time. The most famous volcano, although inactive, was the scenic Mount Fuji.

Of course, learning about Japan from my perspective meant representing it, so I brought many things to school: chopsticks with inlaid bits of mother-of-pearl, folding fans, porcelain rice bowls, lacquerware. I soaked up the knowledge presented in that unit like a sponge, for it was all relevant *to me* and I would never forget it. Something else formed, too: pride. The Japanese were an extraordinary people who made exquisite and beautiful works of art. And I was one of these people.

The pride swelled and grew until the day the unit ended. Abruptly. The next thing I knew, the map of Japan on the wall was replaced with Australia's. And although I learned all the states and capitals of that country, discovered the marvels of the Great Barrier Reef, and had a taste of some amazing turtle soup, I never felt quite the same about Australia.

When the unit on Japan was over, I was told to take all the things I had brought to school home in a large paper bag. At that time, I rode a school bus back from Old Town through to New Town. That day, the bus broke down midway through its route, and I was forced to walk home. Jostling that bag from one arm to the other, stopping to rearrange its contents or fold over the top so I could get a better grip, made me think that what had once made me so proud was now a burden.

Mom was a Christian. She was baptized as a young woman in Osaka in postwar Japan, an abysmal and wretched time for many people. Although my mother's family escaped relatively unscathed—her father had come back, after all, from Indonesia—she was not immune to the general conditions of the time. People were hungry, jobs were scarce; it was a joyless time.

During the Occupation, the Americans sought to boost the

general state of the defeated nation's morale by infusing it with the vigour of their religious beliefs. A special missionary visa was created, which allowed many American missionaries to come to and start churches in a country whose spiritual energy had been sapped by the emasculating of their divine ruler, the emperor, to the status of a mere mortal.

At that time in Takarazuka, where she lived, my mother saw an American missionary walking around the area. Curious about this *gaijin*—gaijin literally means outsider or foreigner—she kept her eye on him, and saw him disappear into a church. Around the same time, there was an advertisement in the paper for free bibles. Mom ordered one, read a bit of it, and then decided she would follow that gaijin missionary to his church.

No one in the family was Christian; her decision to become one was her own. My grandfather—a cosmopolitan, and university-educated—had no objections. What my grandmother thought, I have no idea. But being fairly well educated herself, I imagine she wasn't opposed to it; the Christians had a legacy of education in the country that was admired by many. The Methodists, for example, had built nearby Kwansei Gakuin University in Nishinomiya, the school and church to which my mother's gaijin missionary was affiliated. Through her church's connection to the school, she would eventually go on to work at the theology department there, while her brother and cousin would be admitted there as students in the late sixties.

My father was not a believer himself; his family was nominally Buddhist but not very observant. He knew my mother was Christian, but did not know how or where to connect her to a church. In Edmonton, Mom had Japanese Christian friends, but in Hay River, she had no one.

So one day, not long after we arrived in Hay River, she set out with me, my toddler brother, and sister in a stroller and headed into New Town to look for a church. There was a large building that looked like a log cabin with a steeple, and we knocked on the door. The priest was there. He was an older man with a shocking amount of white hair. Mom and he talked politely, perhaps the way she might have talked with that American missionary back in Japan. She wanted to know if there was a Sunday school and how one could attend services.

What was that conversation like between my mother and that priest? Was I even used, as sometimes immigrant children are, to conduct a conversation their parents can't carry on their own? *Yes, my mom's looking for God. Does He live here? She wants me to find Him, too. She wants me to go to church.*

I didn't end up going to that Anglican church, after all. The neighbours across the street, the Kirkpatricks, took me instead to their church, the Pentecostal one in town. Everett Kirkpatrick worked with my father at the airport, so Dad must have asked him if he'd take me. I went to church with them, always on my own. Mom never accompanied me; she had to stay home with my brother and sister. One day, however, missionary folk showed up at the door. They gave her a tract, *The Watchtower,* which they also had available in Japanese. They told Mom they would love to visit her at home and have Bible study with her. Yes, Mom agreed. That arrangement would be just perfect.

It was in the Pentecostal church that the god-with-no-name began to take shape. *My God is so Big, so strong and so Mighty, there's nothing He cannot do. The Rivers are His, the Mountains are His, the stars are his handiwork, too.*

Was that the Sunday school song that floated through my mind as I trudged home from school one wintry day in the increasing murk of the late afternoon? It went dark early in the Northwest Territories in winter. I had somehow left the road and gone off course through a shrubby stand of naked wood and deeper snow. Abruptly, I stopped and looked up. In the sky were the northern lights, a shimmery curtain of wavering green and blue. It was unlike anything I had ever seen, except maybe the Alexandra Falls. *The Rivers are His, the Mountains are His, the stars are His handiwork, too.*

42

I stood in the deep snow, its white surface radiant under the light, while below, a cold wetness clung to my legs, shackling me to the wonder. It was not a song I had been singing that led me off course, but rather a story I had been telling myself, imagining myself in it, in such an enthralled and distracted way when, suddenly, I was awakened to where I was at that precise moment.

The snow was glistening, the shrubs naked and black, and the sky aflame with light.

Now *this* was the real world—not the story I was in. And this world was amazing, as if it had been created just for me.

What imparts the mystery of the world and makes it into truth for a child? Song and word. Hymns and scripture memorization are the legacy of the Sundays I attended that Pentecostal church in Hay River. Biblical texts were important at this church, and we were encouraged to memorize long passages of the Bible. I memorized the Gospel of John and recall reciting it to an audience: *In the beginning was the Word, and the Word was with God, and the Word was God. The same was in the beginning with God. All things were made by him; and without him was not any thing made that was made. In him was life; and the life was the light of men.*

I stood in front of a small Sunday school audience in the church basement; there were adults present, not just my peers. A piano was nearby and my Sunday school teacher in the wings, to prompt me, if necessary. In hindsight, I see now that I was chosen because I was exemplary: here was an Asian girl with a prodigious capacity for memorization who was now going to recite from the Gospel of John.

He was in the world, and the world was made by him, and the world knew him not. He came unto his own, and his own received him not. But as many as received him, to them gave He power to become the sons of God, even to them that believe on his name:

Which were born, not of blood, nor of the will of the flesh, nor of the will of man, but of God.

And so, as I memorized and recited, the Word took hold of my soul and made it flesh.

Occasionally, I would see Indigenous people at church. I did not know it at the time, but the Hay River Pentecostal church was a mission church, started in 1949 as the foundational congregation for the Pentecostal Sub-Arctic Mission. It was the first of its denomination to build a church in the Northwest Territories and it would go on to later to build hospitals as well.

My father made sure the community was aware of my minority status in town. He helped me find a church through his colleague at work. When there were major concerts or events in town, he made sure to take me. With him, I heard my first riveting recitation of Charles Dickens's *The Christmas Carol* by an actor brought into town to perform it at the newly built Diamond Jenness High School. By the end of my year in Grade 3, when he was often down to Edmonton on business trips, he'd come back with good Christian books for me to read; this was how I was introduced to Paul White's *Jungle Doctor* series, for example.

In the spring of my year in third grade, there were massive puddles in the schoolyard. I remember a particular incident that stayed with me into my adulthood and about which I eventually wrote a poem. That wet spring, my friends and I cautiously waded into the deepest puddle to the upper rims of our rubber boots, testing our limits as the heavy dark waters pressed against our ankles and calves. All of a sudden, in a great fury and clatter, an Indigenous boy named Rocky came splashing into the puddle with his running shoes on. We stared at him, horrified. He grinned back, triumphant—a mouth full of missing teeth, his stubbly black hair sticking up from his head, and eyes shaped like crescent moons.

He did not give a care in the world. It was as if he could walk on water. Rocky standing in that puddle up to his knees became a poem, incarnate in my imagination just as it was written: *And so was the Word made flesh and dwelt among us, and we beheld his glory, the glory as of the only begotten of the Father, full of grace and truth.*

CHAPTER THREE:

STORY LIKE A HOUSE

The house was full of scribes and storytellers,
and I would hear their talk and read their words.

—Sally Ito

7/25/1975

We arrived at John's new house in Sherwood
Park. It was bigger and grander than I could have
imagined.

Sherwood Park was a suburb of Edmonton,
about a 25–30 minute drive from Edmonton's
downtown. When I was visiting here last, this area
would have all been bush and farm fields; it did
not have a community name. Now, on the maps,
there was a community name with streets and
boulevards. Sherwood Park was a luxurious residential suburb with big houses of varying design.
Many of these houses were split level with first,
second, and half storeys, and basements. When
I say 'three storeys' this did not include the basement. Because Akiko's house was on a slope, the
house was designed to take advantage of its position there. When you entered the house from the

front entrance, there was one level that had a bedroom and family room. A few stairs upwards, and you were on the second level, which had the living room, dining room, kitchen, and laundry room. Then there was a regular staircase up to the second floor that had three bedrooms. There were two bathrooms and half-bath downstairs on the first level. Next to the front entrance to the left was a double garage. This house was at least sixty tsubo and felt very spacious. It was incomparably bigger than the last house I'd seen them in. The yard, I guessed from observation, was about 250–300 tsubo. Akiko and John's house was typical of the kind that lined Manchester Drive. People who lived here were doctors, lawyers, company presidents. John had bought this house for $65,000, the Japanese price equivalent of which you could not buy any house comparable to this, or so I thought.

The population of Sherwood Park was to be restricted to 25,000. There were three elementary schools, three junior high schools, and two shopping centres. The cost of living was slightly more expensive than the city. There was one golf course. There was no hospital as of yet. There was a community gym, a skating arena, a swimming pool—the type of recreational facilities white people cannot do without.

So wrote my grandfather, Toshiro, in his travel diary, of our family's house. We moved into it in 1975, two years after our return from the Northwest Territories. This house I considered my childhood home. Located on the western edge of Sherwood Park in an area called Mills Haven, Manchester Drive was a short, crescent-like street that curved gently, following what apparently was a former creek's path down a gradual slope.

At the time, Dad, who was into various investment schemes involving real estate and stocks, alongside his regular federal government job, where he'd been advanced according to his seniority, was flush with cash and could afford a larger home for the family. But the real reason Dad wanted a bigger house was to host relatives from Japan. He'd been planning a trip whereby members of both sides of the family, Saito and Ito, would visit us for about a month in the summer. From my mother's side would come her father, Toshiro Saito, her sister, Yoko Ohkubo, and her sister's ten-year-old daughter, Yumi. From my father's side would come his mother, Chiyoko Ito, and his youngest brother, Hifumi.

That summer of 1975 was the biggest assembling of family members from Japan to visit our house, and it was a significant event. I was very excited. When the day arrived for us to pick them up at the airport, I wanted to be the first to greet them. Unfortunately, just as the plane landed and they were to disembark, my younger sister had to go to the bathroom. I was told to take her. By the time we were done, the relatives were in a huddle already at the foot of the stairs, and I joined the happy, reunited throng belatedly. Missing them at that crucial moment of their arrival made me feel *kuyashi*, frustrated, at having lost an opportunity to witness what I felt in my bones to be a crucial dramatic event. Years later, I was finally able to translate my grandfather's account of the event. In a diary entry dated July 25, 1975, he wrote in his typical, pithy manner:

> I arrived at the Edmonton International Airport and was surprised to see how developed the airport and Edmonton was. Akiko was tearful and embraced me. Then Yoko got weepy, too. Really, it was quite unlike Akiko to cry like that.

So my childish intuition was true! I had missed something after all, and now the writing of it fills me with wistfulness. Writing allowed me to *imagine* what it was like, beyond just being present and recording the facts, like my grandfather. The *imagining* was what launched me into words anyway. The *imagining* was more powerful.

At that time, I didn't really know these relatives very well. This visit, however, would change that. I would get to know them so well, I would not forget them. And when they had gone, their stories would linger, occupy nooks and crannies of memory, and then, like coals about to go out, flare suddenly into a recollected burst that would set off a string of associations like a firework exploding into an array of light. The house was full with Saitos and Itos, both the scribes and the storytellers, and I would embark on a journey of discovery while overhearing their talk and reading their words.

My mother's father, Toshiro Saito, was a tall, elegant man with a thin, long face and fair complexion. In his younger days, as he writes in his memoir, he thought himself handsome:

> In my family, we had very fair skin. When I was a baby, my cheeks were as red as apples and my lips red as crimson flowers, and so this was in quite a contrast to my white complexion; I was said to be a very cute baby by all. Even now in my old age, my lips are still red and I have few age spots. Perhaps this is presumptuous of me to say, but I was raised being told I was a 'pretty boy.' When I became an adult, in Tokyo I would be called a "handsome man"; in Kansai, a "good-looker"; either way I did not like being referred to in this manner. These comments invariably came from older women.

Cosmopolitan, university-educated, and well read, my grandfather was an urbane and sophisticated Japanese gentleman. He brought a journal—a brown, fabric-covered hardback notebook—and took it everywhere on our travels that summer, along with his ever-present camera. He wrote in this book almost daily, making observations about our family and recording events and happenings.

Over forty years later, I would be the one handling the book again, my eyes resting on his finely scripted handwriting, trying with the help of friends and family to translate his words in a writerly attempt to recover the man and his interpretation of my family.

My other living grandparent, Chiyoko, was now in the same house as Toshiro. I hardly knew her at all, for she had not set foot on Canadian soil since her forced expatriation to Japan in 1946. She came with my uncle, her youngest son, Hifumi. Before they left Japan, it was Hifumi who handled the tickets, coordinated the meeting between them and my mother's branch of the family in Japan, and managed the luggage. When they arrived in Vancouver, however, my grandmother took over, trotting out her rusty English, taking charge of things in a manner Hifumi had never seen his mother display before. Clearly, she was in her own element in the country she had known as home for much of her life. Chiyoko, in fact, had been born a stone's throw away from the airport when the town of Richmond was but a collection of silty islands in the Fraser River delta, lined with canneries and docks. The first sounds of the ocean to enter Chiyoko's ears were from the Canadian side of the Pacific, much different from the other side from which her parents had come. When she arrived at our house in Sherwood Park that day, her sister, my Auntie Kay, came out to welcome her. Now, for this brief interval, Auntie Kay, who had always been like a grandmother to me, would be supplanted by my real grandmother. Auntie Kay's role in my eyes shifted. And for Kay, too, the roles had shifted. Now, she was reunited with her older sister, and was in the position of being the host to the one to whom she would defer. She would call her *Neh-san*, which was the respectful term for "older sister." And my grandmother, for her part, would call Kay by her proper Japanese name, *Kiyoe*.

Kiyoe and Neh-san had been through a lot together, especially in the years from 1941 to 1946. They had much to talk about. As my grandfather meticulously recorded in his journal of the visit on the first night of their arrival: Kay and her older sister Chiyoko chattered all night long in the adjoining bedroom and I could not sleep.

Kiyoe and Neh-san were not the only sisters reunited on this trip. There was also my mother and her sister, Yoko, who had brought her ten-year-old daughter, Yumi, with her.

Yoko was my mother's younger sister. Only two years apart, they shared a history of sisterhood in Japan I knew little about. By the time I met her and Yumi, the two women had spent years apart in their respective countries. But like Kiyoe and Neh-san, their relationship as siblings was forged in good part during the war.

Mother was nine, the oldest child in the family during the worst of the war years, with an absent father, and was saddled with the care of her two younger siblings. As the oldest child, she became strong, bossy, and assertive. But not so much the second child. Yoko was mild, meek, and, perhaps, a touch oversensitive. She was always considerate of other people's feelings—a good thing—but when overextended, she could become resentful and withdrawn. It was easy to take advantage of her kindness and generosity without realizing it, as I would later discover on trips in my adult years to Japan, and, with her particularly, the Japanese concept of *amae*—a difficult word to translate, roughly meaning the kind of selfless dependence a child feels for his/her mother—would play a factor in my encounters with her.

My mother and her sister: one went to Canada, and one stayed. But each had their own desires and ambitions, which they spoke of and shared with one another and of which I had no understanding as a child. On this trip with children and relatives underfoot and everywhere, my grandfather was awakened to a revelation given to him by his daughters:

7/29

At lunch, we three ate together and conversed happily. It was the first time since Yoko had left our family to be married that I had spent such a long time with her—a month and a half—in Canada, and so I felt I got to know her better here. With Akiko, whenever she came to Japan, she spent at least two and a half months with me at my house so I was already familiar with her personality. This time, my two daughters revealed to me that they felt that their younger sister Michiko had been highly favoured by me because she had been sent to a private Catholic girls high school and went to the famous Doshisha University for a four-year degree, thus receiving a much better education than they had. I was unaware of their feelings about this situation and so this was surprising to me.

Alongside a reunion of sisters would be one of brothers. Hifumi was the sixth and last son of the Ito family, a postwar baby brought up in postwar Japan. He was the son conceived and born in Japan. As the American transport ship, the *General Meigs*, left the harbour at Vancouver with a shipload of 1,100 repatriates in 1946, my grandmother, with her husband and their five boys, was among them. In a mood of unhappy resignation, my grandmother must have attributed the queasiness she felt in her stomach to stress, not pregnancy. This child she miscarried soon after her arrival, but now on Japanese soil, she found herself pregnant again, this time with Hifumi.

Hifumi could have easily been a Canadian child if things had gone differently, if different choices had been made. But he was born in Japan and raised entirely in that country. Canada, though, was an echoing and haunting presence in his life, filtered through his mother and older brothers' experiences there. He was curious about where his mother had come from, and curious about how his older brothers, Tom and Stan, had fared in the country of their birth. My father was the first to return to Canada and sponsored two of his younger brothers to come later. Was life better in Canada? Had the older brothers who forged their destinies in Canada been successful?

When Hifumi was born, my father was twelve, exiled with his family to a country he did not know. They lived in a ramshackle farmhouse with a dirt floor in Oiwake, Mie Prefecture, on a parcel of land given them by their uncle in nearby Aichi Prefecture. This land was adjacent to a former airstrip for the Japanese military. The airstrip was dismantled and decommissioned by the Occupation Forces, and the land parsed out into plots to be given to wartime returnees from abroad, mostly from Manchuria. The land was rock-hard and not particularly arable. Although my grandparents were returnees, they were not part of the contingent who received land through this scheme, although my grandfather did join their cooperative to get better prices on farm implements. The family was, in fact, the only returnees from North America—the land of the former enemy—and was therefore singled out as such by being referred to as the *Yankees*. The term was pejorative.

Going from being the "Jap" in one country to the "Yankee" in another must not have been pleasant. No matter where they went, the Ito family felt like perpetual outsiders. And by virtue of being the son of his Canadian mother, Hifumi was a Yankee too.

Of all the relatives who came, only one was close to my age: my cousin Yumi. She was Japanese and therefore different from North American me. Her straight black hair was tidily kept in pigtails while mine was quickly swept into a ponytail. She wore skirts and blouses. She played the piano as seriously as I pursued figure skating. There was a summer figure skating school in Sherwood Park at the time and I was enrolled in it; figure skating was the only activity I ever wore a skirt for at that age.

Yumi didn't speak any English and my Japanese wasn't very

good. But in the way of children, we learned to get along, or that, at least, is how my grandfather recorded it in his diary on July 29:

> As for the kids playing with each other, Sally, Daniel, and Cathy could understand what Yumi was saying. And Yumi seemed to understand their English, so they played well together.

However, he also did record, curiously enough, this observation:

> At the shopping centre, Yumi was acting so overexcited that I told her, "Look, you're the oldest one here." But Sally tapped me on the hand, pointed to her nose to indicate that she, in fact, was the oldest. This was true, but Yumi was taller. However, Sally was the oldest, and so gradually everybody began to follow her and copy her style and pace of leadership. Sally never listened to what her parents told her. She would talk back to Akiko constantly. No doubt, she had her reasons for disagreeing with every-thing, but this drove Akiko crazy.
>
> Last time I was here, I could understand the children's English but this time I couldn't under-stand a word they were saying. However, observing Sally's attitude, I did not like her.

The irony of my reading this passage over forty years later struck me as something I deserved. However, as I would discover in further reading, my grandfather's observations of the personal-ities and relationships of various family members would help illu-minate much of what, for me, was either opaque or merely taken for granted, especially on our forthcoming car trip through the Rockies to the West Coast and back.

CHAPTER FOUR:

DRIVE

I did not sleep but stayed awake to encourage the driver.

—Toshiro Saito

Last night I had a dream. Auntie Kay and I were in a car together, and I was telling her I was writing a book. Sometimes Auntie Kay was driving, and sometimes I was. In the dream, there was a child in the back of the car.

Sometimes, as the writer, I think I control the car, while at other times, it is someone else. It is the past, the ghost of someone who lived, the ancestor. Other times, it is the future who drives the car and compels the story to unfold, reveal itself, become testament. It is the infant, the living descendant, the unformed child in the back.

Drive, Auntie Kay says, when I, the writer, can't do it. *Drive*, says the infant in the back.

That summertime visit of my relatives in 1975 was to culminate in a long car trip, meticulously planned out by my father, that would take us westwards through the Rockies, through interior British Columbia, into Vancouver, and back again. We would ride in two vehicles: one driven by my father, and the other by his younger brother Stan. The trip would send us in a backward loop through time, shuttling my father's family through the years of his childhood. It would take the Ito sisters back through a journey of commitments they made to each other before, during, and after the war when the men in their lives were taken away and could no longer exercise family authority. It would take us into the terrain of their exile: the men to lonely road camps, the women and children to tarpaper shacks in the snow.

Toshiro was the unappointed scribe of the journey. A seasoned documenter-of-all-things, he was used to travelling and recording his thoughts and observations. Through the words of his diary of the time, I found my own tunnel into my family's past. While his tourist's eye would be for the monumental majesties of nature, mine would be for the snaking trails of memory that wound through the countryside. I would hear voices—Auntie Kay's mostly, although sometimes others'—which I would faithfully record as my grandfather Toshiro did in his diary so long ago.

The trip began on August 3, and my grandfather records it thus:

8/3

Akiko got up at five o'clock. I got up, too, and went downstairs. After breakfast, we departed in two cars at 8:10. In the car John was driving, the back seat had been turned into a flat space with an air mattress and sleeping bags laid out for the children. Yoko and Akiko sat in the front with John driving. In Stan's car, Hifumi and I sat in the front, Kay and Sanjiro and Chiyoko in the back. This was to be our seating order for the rest of the trip. From there, we would travel together on the highway west. Unfortunately, it was raining when we set out but just past the junction to Whitecourt, the clouds broke and the sun shone through beautifully, opening up the sky into an azure blue. Just before arriving in Jasper National Park, we pulled into a campsite to have lunch. There were many other trailers and campers stopped there as well. We ate onigiri that Akiko had made the night before. The white people around us seemed to be watching what we were eating with interest.

Once we passed Hinton, I noticed the strangely shaped mountains in the distance thru the car window. The road then became more hilly, and we could see snow- and glacier-covered mountains intermittently as we ascended and descended on the road. And so we drove further into the mountains even past Jasper. The plan for the evening was to stay in a place called Avola. When I found it on the map, it appeared to be an isolated little town. When I asked why we were stopping in such a place, Stan said, "Because it's cheap." "I see," I said. An hour past Jasper, we saw a Japanese man stranded on the road, his vehicle having fallen into a deep pool of water that was a result of highway construction. He was probably waiting for the CAA or some other help, and since we didn't have any room, we passed him by. Seeing as it was a Sunday, there might not be any help available.

As I read this section of Toshiro's travel diary, I was startled to see a stranded Japanese man right about where I knew Japanese-Canadian men had been working in road camps after having been forcibly moved from the West Coast. Japanese Nationals like my grandfather, Shigeru Ito, and Auntie Kay's first husband,

Charlie Imahashi, built the highway we were on, the Yellowhead, which snaked through the Rockies in Alberta southwards to Kamloops. A voice of a Japanese man, that of my paternal grandfather, Shigeru, began speaking in my head, as if addressing us from the murky past.

August 1942

Wait, stop! Why won't they stop? They look Nihonjin.

I'll tell them who I am. Because I'm Nihonjin, too. A worker sent here for road construction with all them other Nihonjin, or "Japs" as the hakujin like to call us. Up there, just behind those trees, there is the camp I'm in. They brought us in on the railway from Vancouver and we were housed in bunk cars until we built ourselves a camp. We're supposed to be building roads.

Well, at least I'm here with Imahashi. He's my brother-in-law, Kiyoe's husband. We came here together. A good man, but not of strong constitution. That's why he was doing the bookkeeping for the Buddhist church. But I guess as far the authorities are concerned he's still as much a threat as the other of us Nihonjin men are. "Enemy aliens," that's what we're called. The other men of the family—my Uncle Saichi, and Jack—they went to southern Alberta to those sugar beet farms. Don't know what's going to happen with them there.

Truth be told, I don't even know what's happening to Chiyoko or the boys. Imahashi and I—we just had to leave our farms so suddenly.

The mountains here are bigger than Japan's. Everywhere around us is bush. And the nights are cool, even in midsummer.

They want us to build roads here to connect the rest of the province to the coast. That's what they say, anyway, but there isn't really much work. Mostly, we sit around. They pay us but not very much, and then they deduct what it costs to keep us here. What use is this road we're supposed to be building? What is it going to be for anyway? It was just an excuse for the authorities to get us Nihonjin off the coast.

I feel like a prisoner.

My grandfather Toshiro continues the next day:

8/4

At six, we wake up. Today's drive will be the longest; we will be going to White Rock, BC, on the Pacific coast. Looking on the map, I see that we are travelling from the farthest point east in the province to the farthest west. It's about 370 miles, which is about 600 km. If the road was good and we drove at the maximum of sixty miles per hour, we would reach our destination in about ten hours non-stop, but factoring in breaks and stops, it might take twelve or thirteen hours.

Evening fell and we were still on our way to Hope. By now the sun was setting. It was 8:00 and my back was sore from the long drive. In order to avoid sleepiness, drivers were switched. Hifumi took over for John and John slept deeply. Then Hifumi went back to Stan's car, slept, and then switched off with Stan so Stan could sleep. I did not sleep but stayed awake to encourage the driver.

The sun went down, and the western sky sunset of Vancouver came into view. Our destination of White Rock was off Highway 1. John's mother, Chiyoko, and Kay said they had worked around in this area when they were young, harvesting hops.

As I read these words in this entry of Toshiro's diary, I hear Auntie Kay's voice:

Neh-san, remember those days? When the valley was filled with fields and gardens and we picked and harvested everything green and lovely to eat? Of course, we did strawberries like everyone else, but there were other things grown like tomatoes, and fruit trees, and hops, too. So many Nihonjin farmers in the valley, there was always somewhere we could find work! That's why I told you that you should run away. Remember that? When Papa said he was bringing Shigeru from Japan to be your husband? That no-good cousin of yours you never liked when Papa sent you as a girl to his brother's house for your education? It was you yourself who told me cousin-marriages were no good; you were reading that in those newfangled Japanese women's magazines only you could read. "Cousins should not marry. There could be birth defects in the children." You read that line out loud to me. And of course, there was Maeno, too. That boy down the road; he sure liked you! Papa didn't know about that. He was in Japan, anyway, planning your future without any of your say in it. But shikata ga nai, neh? That is the way of things. Except, I don't really believe that, Neh-san, do you? What if you ran away? You could work harvesting hops for that farmer like last summer. Work there, save up some money, and then maybe you and Maeno could ... could ... there's an English word for running away to get married. I remember it now. Elope.

And my grandfather's voice again:

8/5

We stayed at the Bay Apartment Motel in White Rock, which we arrived at late at night. When I woke up in the morning, I looked outside and could see the beach right in front of us. The tide was completely out and in the far distance were the ocean waves beyond.

Everyone went out to go shellfish hunting in the low tide. We found large ones that looked like akagai, cockles. Auntie Kay had often gone shellfish hunting here in the past but had never seen such large cockles. She said, "Before, when we Nihonjin lived here, we were always looking for shellfish, so maybe they never got a chance to get this big."

Auntie Kay remembered:

Neh-san, how oiishi the akagai are! How lucky to harvest them from the ocean again. Remember when we used to come down here for fishing and picnics and kai-tori? The tide was so far out today, and the sun shining—the weather was perfect—and we could all go out like we used to back when we lived in Surrey—John, Stan, Hifumi—and Sally, too, she's got a shell collection, you know, so this was a perfect day for her. I told her we used to come down to White Rock when we could as a family. I wanted John to take us here, because we have such good memories of this place. He must remember, too. Jack and Papa used to take the boys fishing. And remember the chombogai we'd dig up? That ugly shell with the chimpo coming out like a man's you-know-what? Well, you know, the chimpo was the best part to eat, but it took such a lot to dig them out of the muck, they were so deep in. Men's work, neh, to get them out? Heh, heh. And then we women would clean it, prepare it, and eat it. But today, I've never seen it like this, those akagai coming in with the tide, so easy to get—you could just scoop them up with your hand like baseballs rolling in from the sea. Mezurashii. How amazing, the sea!

~

8/6

I slept in until eleven. Since we weren't travelling and didn't have to load or unload the car, we set out for sightseeing at once, knowing we would return to the same motel. We were going to visit Surrey, the old hometown of the Ito family. When Chiyoko and Auntie Kay had lived in Surrey, it was mostly farmland and bush with the odd house built here and there. Now it had become a city with suburban residences all lined up in a row; in effect, it had become a suburb of Vancouver. We went looking for an old friend of the Itos, the Moriokas, whose address we looked up in the phone book the night before. They no longer lived at this address anymore, however. So then we went looking for a cousin of Kay's first husband, Imahashi-san, and after getting lost and driving around, we found them. This cousin was just over fifty years old and he remembered John's mother. Of course, he knew who Auntie Kay was. He invited us in to his place, and there he told us that he ran a mushroom-growing operation that had been quite successful and profitable. He confirmed to us where the old Ito residence was and so, taking our leave, we got into the cars and headed off to the old homestead. Some of the buildings were still there, and the usually quiet and expressionless Chiyoko suddenly became talkative and weepy as she and her sister gazed at the sight of their old home.

~

So, let me tell you about the farm, Sally. Papa bought eighty acres of land on Sandell Road in Surrey in about 1926. It was all wooded then, except for about ten acres, so he had to clear it. In those days, you used dynamite to clear the land, the trees were so big. Then the men would come and haul out the logs by horse and cart. The trees made everything dark so when they were taken down, the farm felt sunnier, brighter.

The Nihonjin, they all helped each other. You'd hear the sound of dynamite going off all over the neighbourhood, and you knew somebody was clearing their land that day, either of stumps or trees. Some of the trees were cedar, which smelled really fine, and you could make good use of the wood for building materials for your house and outbuildings.

After the land was cleared, we grew strawberries and rhubarb, and raised chickens, too. We had rows of strawberries—big, bright green mounds of leaves with juicy, red berries under them. They were sweet and delicious. The hakujin liked them with cream and sugar, and they made things like strawberry shortcake, which we learned to make, too. Neh-san and I, we would go down the rows together and pick fast—you never pull off the green leaf part of the strawberry when picking, but snip off the stalk just above the berry with a sharp fingernail. When we finished a row, we'd go to the next one, but sometimes I'd stop and have a stretch. You could see all these rows of plants going off into the distance, and I'd think, "Holy! How am I going to pick all those?" Pickers weren't supposed to eat the strawberries, but sometimes, I'd eat one or two. Neh-san never ate any. It's funny, the feelings you have when you grow a crop for money. You stop wanting them somehow and think of the things you can buy instead with the money, but I never stopped wanting to pick berries and eat them or make jam or freeze them. Neh-san would buy books or magazines to read with her money.

We also raised chickens, like a lot of our neighbours. We Nihonjin were good at chick sexing; in fact, Papa wanted Shigeru to learn how to do it when he came to Canada, because there were some expert chick sexers already working in Surrey at the time. You wanted the pullets for the eggs, but if you didn't separate the pullets from the cockerels, then the males would make life miserable for the females, so they had to be separated out. That was the job of the chick sexer.

The farm we all started out on was on Sandell Road, but eventually, after we both got married, we spread out in the area, but not too far from each other. Chiyoko worked so hard, she had enough money to build her own house. It was on Papa's land, but it was her house. I lived with Charlie not too far away. He was farming land he bought from his brother. We grew strawberries and rhubarb and had chickens, too. The chickens made good manure for fertilizing the fields. We were always on hand to help each other out, and all the other Nihonjin, too, in the area; we did things together like picking berries, going to the Buddhist church, going to picnics and swims at White Rock.

Our neighbours in the area were the Maenos, the Inouyes, the Moriokas, the Imahashis, and the Sunadas. The Maenos were from Aichi-ken, like Papa, and they had three daughters and a boy. That boy, he liked Neh-san a lot and was always coming round to see her. I think he wanted to marry her. But Papa had already picked Shigeru for her when he was in Japan visiting his mother, so it was too bad for her. Neh-san had spent a long time in Japan as a girl—she was older than Jack and I—so when she came back, we hardly knew her. I had to teach her English all over again.

Papa got to know the Imahashis through the Buddhist church. When Papa was fishing, he'd take risks with his boat, going out into storms when no one else would. He would catch a lot of fish, and then he'd make a big donation to the Buddhist church. My husband, Ichiro, or "Charlie," worked as treasurer for the church, and that's how I got introduced to him. Charlie was a yobi-yose—you know, those boys whose relatives call them over from Japan? Anyway, he was from Kochi. He was a gentleman and kind. We got married in 1937.

Jack, he fell in love with Molly Sunada. Her papa was a real leader in the community and was active in the berry growers' association. The Surrey Berry Hall was on Sandell Road; it had its own private telephone line and was a busy place during berry season. After the berries were harvested, they'd be brought in by truck to the hall where they were stamped with numbers assigned to us growers. Then the trucks would drive them off to Vancouver to market. Farmers' trucks could go for free on the Patullo Bridge that was over the Fraser River.

I was sad when Jack married Molly. Jack was my big brother, and I loved him a lot. But Molly, she was a good wife for him. I owe her a lot. She took care of everybody, even Neh-san's kids—John, Stan, and Tom—when they come back to Canada.

One of my friends in Surrey was Beverley Inouye. She was the daughter of a First World War vet who was injured in battle. You would think that would count for something, but when it came time for us to evacuate, he had to go, too. He was put in Hastings Park like us. I heard he threw his medals in anger on a desk somewhere, saying, "Is this what I fought for in this country? To be treated like this?"

I had another friend; she was a Christian and she went to that English church on Old Yale Road on the hill. Sometimes she'd ask me if I would like to come. At first, I said no. You see, when I was younger, Neh-san and I would cut through that church's graveyard on the way back from the train station when we went to town. One time we were coming home and it was getting dark, and we had to go through the graveyard. Well, it was so darn spooky that Neh-san grabbed my hand and we ran through that yard as fast as our legs could take us.

That church was on the hill and it had a tower

built beside it; there was a light in it that you could see from the river, and the fishermen used it to find their way.

Charlie and I, we wanted to have kids, but I couldn't have any. I think the trouble was with me. I got my period late; I was almost nineteen, so something wasn't right about my body for making babies. Maybe Neh-san was right: Mama and Papa were cousins, and maybe because of that I had no period. A birth defect. But Neh-san, even though she was small, she was fertile. After she got married to Shigeru, she had five boys—boom— one after the other. They got their English names from the hakujin doctor in New Westminster—John, Jim, George, Tom, and Stanley. But Neh-san called them by their Japanese names: Kunitaro, Toshiyuki, Takashi, Shiro, Nobu. I called them by their English names. Stan, the youngest one, he had a caul when he was born. Neh-san was always worried about her boys having birth defects, so she was always checking them when they were born. She wanted me to keep my eye on him.

I went to her place often. The boys would be running around like hellions when I'd go over there. Dishes were piled up in the sink, and laundry scattered all over, and I'd say to one of the boys, "Where's your mother?" And they would point outside, and there she was, way at the end of the garden, hoeing away without a care in the world.

Life in Surrey was good. But then came the war. Everything changed overnight.

It started, of course, on December 7, 1941, with the bombing of Pearl Harbor. People heard about it on the radio and the news spread like wildfire throughout Surrey. "What is going to happen to us?" people were wondering. Right away, the navy took all the fishing boats to the dyke near New Westminster. We could see them from up on the hill in Surrey—hundreds and hundreds of boats. Papa wasn't a fisherman anymore, but he could tell the boats, the way they were rounded up like that, it wasn't good for them, jostling like that against each other. He wondered, "What are they going to do with them?" Those boats were livelihoods.

Then they closed the Japanese schools. Good riddance, I say. What do the kids need to know Nihongo for, anyway? But Neh-san, not only could she speak Nihongo but she could read it, too, and sometimes I envied her. She spoke to the boys in Nihongo, but they went to the English school like all the other kids.

The men in the family—Charlie and Shigeru—registered as Japanese Nationals with the Registrar of Enemy Aliens. This seemed like a normal thing to do at the time since Japan was at war, but then later they asked all of us Nisei to register, too, which seemed a little wrong, seeing as we were born here, but I guess, to the hakujin, we all wore the enemy's face. I got a registration card that I was to show in public places, but I didn't use it much since I wasn't going anywhere.

December was not a good month for us; everything was so uncertain. Then in January, we got word that everyone was to be evacuated. "But where?" we wondered. There were so many rumours, so much talk. The Japanese-language papers had closed, and there was only the New Canadian left to tell us what was going on. The men were to go to road camp, someone said, and then someone else said that farmers were needed for the sugar beet farms in southern Alberta. It was Papa who decided what we would do. He said he and Mama would go with Jack and Molly to the sugar beet farms. Jack and Molly had only two children, Mariko and Toshiko. That would mean there would be the four adults to work the land. I said I wanted to go, too. Charlie and I were a couple; we could work in the fields, too, but Papa said, "No, you stay with your older sister. She's got all those boys to look after."

Not long afterwards, the RCMP came to get our vehicles. Jack had to give up our truck we used to haul berries to market and Charlie and I had to give up our truck, too. It was like losing a fishing boat. Someone saw all the trucks go over the Patullo Bridge at once like it was a parade. They told us we'd get the trucks back once we'd been evacuated somewhere. Neh-san and I wondered if that were really true.

Jack and Molly, Papa and Mama, left for Alberta. Just like that, it was so quick.

Charlie and Shigeru were going to be taken to road camp, for sure. The authorities had their names already because they were Japanese Nationals. They took to hiding out in the woods for a while at the back of the property, but they couldn't stay out there like that forever, so they gave themselves up to the RCMP and were taken to a train station to go to a road camp. We didn't know where they were going or when they would come back. Papa was right; Neh-san was alone now and needed help. It was just me and her and the boys left on the farm. She and I, we worked hard to help each other. She helped me take my furniture and things to store at Papa's. We'd ordered some chicks—1,500 for spring to raise in the coming year. We paid for them but only had them for a few days; after the evacuation order went out and everyone started leaving, the chick seller came back to our farm to take them away. Neh-san and I just stood there and watched the hakujin herd the chicks into the cages and load them onto the truck. Even the boys stood with us and watched. I was so mad, but Neh-san, she looked at me and shrugged. Shikata ga nai, she said. The boys were quiet for a change. They knew something was going on. I could hear the chicks chirping in the back of that truck, until the driver started up the engine. Then it was so loud, I couldn't hear them anymore, and the boys, well, they chased that truck to the end of the driveway, yelling the whole time until the truck disappeared down the road.

A couple of days later, we got notice that the RCMP were going to take us to Hastings Park in Vancouver. We didn't do anything but hide out in the house. What had we done that was so wrong, anyway? They could come and get us, for all I could care. We weren't going anywhere anyhow, unless someone forced us.

~

8/6

After visiting Surrey, we drove into downtown Vancouver on King George Highway and went to a shop in Gastown that had Chinese and Japanese foodstuffs. This shop carried all sorts of other Japanese goods as well, such as magazines, books, and other lifestyle goods. Here, I bought some kazunoko herring roe. Everything here was expensive.

It was now time for lunch. John wanted to take us to a favourite Chinese restaurant he liked. Auntie Kay paid for this meal because she had profited well from her strawberry sales back home in Redwater. Then we went to Stanley Park, and the UBC campus grounds, and Queen Elizabeth Park.

~

Neh-san and I, we went to Vancouver now and then, before we both were married. Or sometimes I went with Jack in the truck when he hauled berries to the market. We'd cross the Patullo Bridge and see the muddy, brown Fraser flowing under us and then we'd be on the King George Highway, which took you straight into the city. The berries would be unloaded, we'd get our money, and then we'd go for lunch somewhere, usually in Chinatown or on Powell Street. Powell Street was where all the Nihon-jin were and where the shops were for stuff from Japan. Neh-san would buy her magazines here. And we'd get things like shoyu and nori. Papa and Charlie would go to the Buddhist church; it was on Alexander Street, same street as the language school. Sometimes, if we planned our visit right, we'd catch an Asahi baseball game at Oppenheimer Park. Jack and Papa were real fans.

I used to look forward to going to Vancouver. It was the big city. But the day the RCMP came to get us to take us to Hastings Park was the end of all those feelings for me. We were given only a few hours' notice so Neh-san and I had to pack quickly. We took suitcases with clothes, and some kitchen items—oh, the dishes, it was so hard to part with them! Mama left her chawanmushi set in the house when they went to Alberta. If you can, Kiyoe, she said to me, save them. She used them at New Year's mostly, and because we raised chickens, the cha-wanmushi custard was always so tasty! I decided to wrap them up and take them. Maybe someday I would have a chance to give them back to her. Neh-san had a suribachi she used all the time for grinding sesame seeds; it was big and brown, with nice grooves in it; we decided to take that. It was large but useful. We didn't know what to expect at Hastings Park, whether we would be able to cook or not, but we wanted to take things with us that we knew we could use wherever we were. The biggest item we wanted to take was our sewing machines. We each had our own, and used them a lot. Papa had won them, gambling. The man he was playing against didn't have any money, so he gave Papa what he had, which were the machines. I guess he wanted to start a business with them. They were top-notch Singers, black frames. So nice, and smooth to use. You'd pump the treadle and run your cloth through—zing!—like that. When the RCMP truck came, Johnny—that's what I called your dad—went up to one of the officers and said, "My mom and aunt want to take their sewing machines because they sew our clothes on them." The officer looked at him, and then at us, and then at the sewing machines. And then he grunted, and said that was fine. Neh-san and I gave each other a look of relief.

Hastings Park was the fairground for the Pacific

National Exhibition. It was east of Powell Street. There was a big set of gates at the entrance, and when we walked through, you could smell livestock and lime. The boys didn't seem so upset; it was a new place for them—fairgrounds, they'd been told—so they thought they could play games all day. Johnny took off like a lightning bolt to find other boys to play with and we were always having trouble finding him afterwards. People already in the park called it the Pool. We met some folk there who had been evacuated from the islands with hardly any notice. Listening to their stories made me realize that there are always people worse off than you.

We were put up in bunks in segregated quarters with blankets between us acting as dividers. Meals were served in the dining hall. They were not very good. We had porridge every breakfast, often with no sugar or milk. Your uncle George hated the stuff even though Neh-san tried to force him to eat it. "Mata kore ka? This stuff again?" He had such a sad look on his face.

The authorities put our big items in a storage building in the park. New people were coming in all the time, so we were worried about our things being misplaced or stolen even. So Neh-san and I would go and look to make sure our sewing machines were still there. One day, Neh-san noticed something new. It was a large stone with a name tag around it. Who would think to bring this? Then Neh-san said, "Tsukemono no ishi da." It's a pickling stone. But of course! The stone was just the right size to put on the wooden disc used to press down the vegetables for making tsukemono. Neh-san and I—we looked at each other and burst out laughing. Surely, such a stone could be found wherever they were sending us. But no matter, you pack whatever you think is important to take with you on a journey.

~

8/8

The plan for today was to go to Kelowna. The sun was shining brightly from the morning. It reflected off the grain fields in jagged flashes of light. It was also very hot. The drivers opened their windows and drove without shirts on, so they could be cooled by the breeze. Before we reached Kelowna, there was a bridge cross-ing over the lake. At the entrance to the city, which was at the foot of the lake, there was a campground and picnic area; even though it was pretty hot out, not that many people were there, maybe because it was still early in the day. Once we entered the city centre, I saw some nice four-storey retirement condos, and a nice residential district. There was another acquain-tance of Auntie Kay's who lived here so Auntie Kay, by recalling the address from the annual Christmas card she received from them, went to visit them, but they were not home. We left a note. On our way out from there, we noticed a greenhouse and nursery so we stopped there. The owner was Japanese, and when he discov-ered that Auntie Kay was a close friend of his neighbour's, he decided to show us around his greenhouse and nursery operation. We could see that he was selling different plants and trees with price tags affixed to them. For Hifumi's sake, as he was interested in gardening, I helped him select some samples of seeds and fruits here, as I had on other places on the trip before. During the war, Auntie Kay, with her previous husband, had worked in the Okanagan Valley near a place called Oyama. During the Meiji period, a Japanese man named General Oyama had come here and the place had been named after him. Whether this was true or not, I wasn't sure. Here, we found a U-Pick cherry orchard. You could eat all you picked and pay whatever extra by weight. This was similar to the way you could go grape picking in Japan. Everyone happily picked cherries. Using ladders, John, Stan, and Auntie Kay got to the higher spots to pick; the other women picked from the lower branches. Freshly picked, these cherries were juicy. They were fresher than the ones from the fruit stands and were more delicious. And they also tasted completely different from the ones sold in stores. They were different from Japanese cherries: bigger, with more fruit on them, and they were a deep burgundy, the colour of cherry brandy. It was the end of the season for cherries in the valley, but it was a bumper crop year. We bought two bucketfuls of cherries and left. Auntie Kay said we could preserve these, but there were still four more days of our trip to go, so it would be hard to keep the cherries fresh for that long. At any rate, Auntie Kay had been feverish about picking cherries. It was not a question, however, of picking them to preserve them, but rather, Auntie Kay enjoyed climbing the tree and picking to her heart's content. This constituted the pleasure of the activity; such a pure spirit of enjoying the moment seemed childlike to me.

~

Neh-san, did I ever tell you how Charlie died, when we were in Oyama? We went there after you and Shigeru went to Japan. Charlie wasn't interested in going to Japan; all his family was staying in Canada. I didn't want to go either. What was Japan to me? I had only been there when I was a kid; I hardly remembered a thing. Neh-san, I felt so bad for you! I know you wanted to stay. I know you cried and fought with Shigeru about it, but he was determined to go back. "They're offering us free passage," he told you. "And we have nothing here, nothing to return to!" That was true. The government sold our properties and we weren't allowed to go back home to the coast. But even so ... Remember how Charlie tried to persuade Shigeru not to go, too? He said, "How can you expect to feed five mouths in Japan after it has lost the war? If it's a matter of feeding your kids, the choice should be obvious." But that Shigeru, he was giving up already. He was feeling sick and tired of the whole thing. His English never got good and he was always giving it to the boys, whacking and yelling at them all the time, although Johnny, he sometimes deserved it, the little rascal. I think Shigeru just wanted to go home. His home, which was Japan. Not yours, of course. Your home was here. Well, at least it was, until we got forced off it.

I know you didn't want to split the family up. You always said that was the worst thing Papa did, sending you to Japan for your education, so that you didn't get to know Jack and me while we were growing up. You told me how terrible it was in Japan, living at Uncle Sentaro's place with all his kids and you having to babysit the little ones all the time. You were supposed to have gone to Mama's relations in Gifu where they didn't have kids, but that didn't work out. No, you always said, it is never a good thing to separate children from their parents. That is the worst possible thing to do. So, of course, you didn't want your boys to be separated from their father. Papa didn't think it was a good idea for you and Shigeru to go to Japan, but he and Jack couldn't have looked after you if you'd stayed with the boys and Shigeru went back. They were just starting all over again in Alberta. In the end, Papa was firm even though he didn't agree with Shigeru. "Do whatever Shigeru wants because he's your husband and you have to obey him now."

Neh-san, kuyashi katta yo. So frustrating! It was hard for you to bear this. But you gave in eventually, because shikata ga nai, neh? That is the way of things in this world.

Still, I never thought that way. I believe you can make your own way in life if you try hard enough. Charlie and I, we decided to go together to Oyama after we left Popoff. Charlie had some relatives out there. We could work, picking fruit out in the orchards there.

When we were in Oyama, Charlie put in a claim with that government Commission named after that judge Bird. Trouble was, we never got paid for the sale of our land in Surrey. The Custodian [Custodian of Enemy Alien Properties] was still holding back money from the sale because they didn't believe we owned it! Charlie had bought it off his older brother years ago, and his brother was stuck in Japan at the time; we never got the deed from him, so when the Custodian went to investigate ownership, the title was still in Charlie's older brother's name. The Custodian sent me letters asking me for receipts for payments made to his brother—one of them even came to me at the Pool right around the time I was in hospital with the mumps—but I didn't have those anymore; the debt had been paid off years ago. Anyway, Charlie and I went to Vernon — it was springtime, I remember; the cherry trees were in bloom—so that he could testify.

But then, that summer, Charlie died. Just like that. I wasn't there when it happened, poor soul; I was high on a ladder, picking cherries, when I saw a man running down the road. He was holding his hat and waving it in the air. I didn't pay much attention to him until he ran closer down the path between the trees waving his hand, calling out to me, "Kay! Kay! Get down from there. It's Charlie—"

Everything up until that moment was fine. It was a perfect sunny day. Me up on that ladder, picking cherries, thinking about nothing.

~

8/9

Today we are going to Slocan and Lemon Creek where the Ito family was interned during the war and where they had painful experiences of being considered enemy aliens. During the war, all Japanese Canadians had to leave the coast for at least one hundred miles, including those born in Canada like the Nisei and Sansei. This was true also of the United States. Childless couples and families with children who were old enough to work were sent into the interior of BC to work in logging or agriculture. Those families with small children, and the elderly, were settled into these small communities like the ones we were visiting. John's elderly grandparents and their son, Jack, and his wife went to work in the beet fields of Alberta; Auntie Kay and her first husband went to Popoff. John's father, who was not of good health, and his mother, with their small children, settled in Lemon Creek until the end of the war. Then, after the war, being disappointed and of low morale, the family decided to return to Japan. The children were new immigrants, although Chiyoko, the mother, was born in Canada, had spent a good portion of her childhood in Japan, and had returned to Canada when she was seventeen, at which point she became a Canadian citizen. At any rate, the family, completely demoralized, resigned themselves to returning to Japan.

In the United States, there was a Japanese-American battalion that fought valorously in Europe, and their patriotism and loyalty to the US were acknowledged by the American government and their land was restored to them. However, in Canada this did not happen, perhaps due to the more British nature of the country, and so the Japanese here were miserable. The Japanese Canadians who survived this period of history recovered through their own hard work and innate abilities.

At the site of the original internment camp, there was nothing but an open field, with prairie dogs leaping about. Probably this was now someone's property: you could see fences and fenceposts around it. We discovered a water pipe coming up from the ground that was from that time. John and Stan had lots of memories of this place. John's mother said there were about 1,500 people living here. When they returned to Japan and met people who were returnees from Manchuria, John's mother said, they knew the conditions in Canada were much better.

A white man came out to greet us. He was the owner of the property. He had grown up as a child in the area and so remembered the Japanese well. He said that Japanese people like John's family would drop in now and then to visit the place.

We stayed around thirty minutes and then left.

~

Just a field now of grass, green and yellow. And the blue mountains behind—"Kootenay Renzan," we called them. It's so peaceful, like a painting. But, Neh-san, so much happened here, it's hard to speak of it all. The boys, they grew up in this field surrounded by these mountains. It was a home for them, the shacks neatly lined up in rows like houses on a street. Look, here are the old railway tracks! Remember how we came here, rattling in on those train cars we got on at the station in Vancouver?

we arrived in early autumn. It felt cooler than on the coast. The scenery was such a change, even beautiful, I'd say. We'd been cooped up in Hastings Park for almost six months. Charlie and Shigeru had returned to us from road camp by then so we were together at least, as families.

Charlie and I signed up for the bunkhouse apartments in Popoff since there were only the two of us. You and Shigeru came here to Lemon Creek because they had shacks here. Rows and rows of them on streets like a village. You were lucky—you got a whole shack to yourself because you had the boys. First time the boys weren't considered a liability, eh, Neh-san? But then you said some people were still jealous. Every other family had to share with perfect strangers. That shack, though, wasn't big enough for you all. The boys were stacked, two to a bunk sometimes, and they were growing. They got underfoot, at least the little ones, Stan and Tom. And Shigeru, I know he had a short fuse, and Johnny was always getting smacked by him. Johnny told me about the gunny sack on the hook on the ceiling and how Shigeru would throw the boys in there when they got to be too much for him. Johnny said it was a good place to read comics, just dangling there, if he had a mind to grab a flashlight beforehand. That boy, he sure was a smart one, but reading in a gunny sack probably ruined his eyes. I know Johnny didn't like sticking around at home with Shigeru around; that's why he was always running off. Home is no place to be when men are idle. That's my conclusion, anyway. Things got better when Shigeru went on garbage detail, although the pay was lousy.

That first winter, remember how cold it was,

Neh-san? And how much snow there was? And so early, too! We'd never seen the likes of it in Surrey! Those shacks weren't insulated at all. Just a bit of tarpaper to cover the surface. You showed me the icicles hanging inside your window—big, gleaming, pointed things like teeth. It took a while to get warmed up, that's for sure; we'd huddle around that pot-bellied stove and put our hands out to the heat and drink plenty of ocha. The older residents told us how bad it had been earlier, what with the water having to be trucked in and having to go all the way to Slocan for the bathhouse, where there were lineups and the water was scummy.

Was it that first winter, Johnny played on the ice on the river, fell in, and nearly drowned? Good thing that boy with the hockey stick saw him!

The Commission [BC Security Commission] took their time getting schools ready. They were building them, but slowly. You and Shigeru couldn't wait. It wasn't good for the boys to be running around like hellions all over the woods. This was true, although Johnny had a good eye for mushrooms. All I'd heard that fall we arrived were rumours about matsutake growing on the mountainside, until Johnny actually found one. So small and white, the cap hadn't even separated from the stem. And it smelled so good, like pine and cinnamon. "Only one?" I asked Johnny, and he shrugged his shoulders and said that was all he could find. "Kuma ga oru zo," you said to him. Yes, there were bears out there. Some of the women who had been huckleberry picking had seen one.

After we got settled in, Johnny would come visit me in Popoff with Jimmy. There'd be a knock on the door, and there he was. "Hi, Auntie Kay, we came to visit you!" and he and Jimmy would plop themselves down and wait for me to give them a treat. Don't be so nice to them, you told me, Neh-san. But what could I do? I couldn't turn them away; they were here already. Anyway, Charlie and I liked their company. We'd play cards with the boys. Sometimes they'd stay late, so I gave them money to take the bus back. Well, that rascal Johnny, I guess he pocketed the money, and Jimmy's, too, and walked home rather than took the bus!

Because that winter was so long, spring was really welcome. The temperatures started warming up and the snow started melting. Near our place, someone noticed fuki buds growing through the snow. I guess you can eat those but I never ate anything but the stalks when the plant was bigger. "Coltsfoot" is the English name for the plant; it looks like rhubarb, but tastes more like celery. The woods were also full of other sansai—spring greens—and people who knew what to look for went out into the woods to go picking. I loved picking warabi, the bracken that grew all over the mountainside. We'd have to cook them good, though, with wood ash, to take out the bitterness.

That spring we heard the Custodian was going to sell our houses and properties on the coast. This was shocking. We thought the Custodian would be keeping our properties for us, not selling them! Our property was being leased to a cooperative for the year so we had a little income coming in from that, but now if they were going to sell it, what would happen to us? Where would we go? How could any of this be true? I dreamt of the farm that night—the rows of strawberries, the rhubarb-forcing house, and the chicken coop and yard, the currant bushes. I picked up a handful of dirt that I thought I threw at a building, but really, I had thrown it into a stream where it melted away like snow. When I woke up, I thought about the farm and about how the strawberry plants and the rhubarb would be budding now and forming new leaves. Who was looking after the farm? Who would the Custodian sell it to? And what would happen to the money after it was sold?

When I thought these thoughts, I grew angry, Neh-san, and clenched my fists and pounded the table. Kuyashikatta yo, neh! It was frustrating.

I never told you, Neh-san, but there was a group of us in Popoff making sake. It started as a casual sort of thing—there was a brewer from Vancouver who knew how to make it. He had the stuff to make the mash with so we would give him trays of steamed rice and he would sprinkle it with the stuff that makes the koji. We had to make the koji in a warm room and had to be pretty careful transporting the mash because making this stuff was illegal, you know. We had to hide it from the RCMP. There was a vat in a back room in one of the bunkhouses, and that's where the final step of filtering took place. When we poured out the first few cups, everyone said "kampai" in not too loud voices, of course, but you know what I said? I said, "Banzai!" Imagine me, a Nisei, saying such a thing!

Well, you know how sake doesn't agree with us Itos. I turned all red right away and felt pretty itchy and sick, so took to bed afterwards. But, you know, I never regretted drinking the stuff and saying what I said, even though it was probably wrong.

By the time the snow was all gone, people were

trying to make their own gardens. You could grow some things here pretty well if you put your mind to it. The Doukhobors had farms in the area and they'd come by in their horse carts to sell vegetables to us. They were nice people, the Russians. I was once invited to tea at Mrs. Popoff's house. I put on a nice dress and a hat, and walked over with the other women she'd invited. These people had fled persecution in Russia, so they knew what it was like to be targeted as a group. Mrs. Popoff felt it was terrible that we Japanese were being treated this way by the Canadian government. But later, when I thought about it, I felt sad, because the Canadian government was paying Mrs. Popoff to put us up on their land, and they were paying them with money the Custodian had received from selling our land on the coast. That's what Charlie said. Remember, he was the treasurer for the Buddhist church? He said we are paying for our stay here with money the government got from the sale of our land.

The Russians grew cabbage and beets, but we wanted to try growing our own vegetables that would be good for making tsukemono. A few of us tried growing daikon. We had a good harvest of them that summer. We couldn't make takuan like they made in Japan, so we tried to pickle them like dill pickles. We'd peel the long white daikon and cut them into rectangular sticks and stuff them into the jars like clothespins. Then we'd pour the oshiru into them, and seal the jars. After a few days, they'd turn yellow from the oshiru, and then we could take them out and eat them with our gohan. They were more crispy than takuan. We called it "denba-zuke," because it was invented in New Denver.

You know, growing your own vegetables, and thinking of ways to eat it, was the pleasure we enjoyed in those days in summertime. The kids played in the river—Johnny taught himself how to swim in Lemon Creek—and there were movies in the hall in Slocan and baseball games, which the RCMP sometimes even joined. We had a sports day with a big picnic. There was even a beauty pageant—imagine being crowned the Queen of Lemon Creek! Anyway, you had to live in the moment and not think too much about the future, because you'd only worry yourself to nothing otherwise. I know some people were concerned about their relatives in Japan; they had no way of knowing what was going on with them over there. But our family, Neh-san, was all here in Canada, except now Papa, Mama, Jack, and Molly and the two girls were in Alberta. They all came out to visit us once just after the government had announced that program for volunteer repatriation. Papa and Mama came with everyone—even the two girls, Toshi and Mariko, in their little hats and woollen coats; someone took a picture of them with the boys. We had a nice time being together like it used to be in Surrey, all things considered. The girls were impressed with the mountains. Johnny and the boys showed them around. In Alberta, they said, it was dry and dusty, the wind blowing all the time. When they left, I felt a little sad. It was nice having the girls around; I missed them. I showed them the scarves I knitted. "It's very cold here in the mountains, girls, much colder than Surrey, so you've got to bundle up!" And then I gave each girl a treat, some candy I bought at the store in Slo-can. You know, Charlie and I, we wanted kids, but we just couldn't have them. When I saw the girls, I felt kuyashi all over again about that business but I didn't tell anyone, not even you, Neh-san. You were always saying you wanted girls, but all you had were boys. We were both out of luck, but in different ways.

Papa had come to try to convince Shigeru to come out west after the war. Repatriation wasn't the only option, he told him. You could move east of the Rockies like the government wanted and go to Alberta. Remember how he said that, Neh-san? For once, Papa was on your side. That was some-thing, don't you think? But of course, Shigeru's mind couldn't be changed.

Charlie and I saw Jack, Molly, and the girls off at the bus stop. When the bus pulled away on the gravel road with them all in it, the dust rising off the road in clouds, I could see the blue mountains in the distance and wished to God I could be some-where else.

~

8/11

We had driven through mountain highways con-tinuously throughout this trip. On one side would be the rock face of the mountain, and on the other, a valley spreading out towards the other face. As we drove, light would be cast onto the road in shafts, depending on the size and shape of the mountain we were driving beside. The mountains continued on like waves. They were like a series of thrones for gods, or like the castles of giants glaring down at one another. As the light of day faded and the mountains went from red to black, they took on the look and feel of ogres, scary and frightening. You could see the layers of rock on the mountains, indicating their millions of years of age and their upward thrust movements into the air. At first, I was amazed at the grandeur of these mountains. The scenery was truly majestic. But later, I grew tired of them. The procession of rock seemed endless. Even if these mountains were like villages of the gods, I was somehow not impressed or filled with grati-tude on looking at them.

CHAPTER FIVE:

HIGH SCHOOL CONFIDENTIAL

●

Japan

Japan

if I say it enough

do you think it'll come true?

—David Fujino

In 1979, I entered high school in Sherwood Park. Salisbury Composite High School was a brown brick behemoth of a building in the centre of the Park, not far from the Sherwood Park Mall and the County of Strathcona administration building, which then also housed the public library in its basement. Not far down the road from Salisbury was its Catholic counterpart, Archbishop Jordan High School. Salisbury was the largest public high school in the area and drew all its students from suburban Sherwood Park and the outlying acreages nearby. The school was two storeys, and because it was a 'composite' high school, it had a vocational wing for subjects such as industrial art, auto mechanics, and typing. Behind the school was a football and track field that stretched out to the west, and the community swimming pool and arena, where I figure skated for many years. At that time, Salisbury was very much a *white* school in its student make-up. I was of but a handful of Asians who went there. There were a few children of mixed Japanese-Canadian heritage with Japanese-Canadian fathers—I could recognize the Japanese last names—but I rarely interacted with these students as I was never in any of the same classes as they were. Neither my mother nor my father knew of these families because my mother's interactions were limited to other Japanese women with younger children living in the Park, most of them Christian, with whom she could more naturally interact in Japanese.

For a long time, I negotiated the divide between the culture and language of the world inside my home and the predominantly white one outside it with the characteristic resilience of childhood, but there were still occasions when my 'otherness' was a target. In junior high, I was called a "Nip," and sometimes when I got on a bus, I was taunted with the song "Chinky, chinky, Chinaman." Kids who came over to my house would say that it smelled like fish, which was ironic: we ate very little fish since my mother preferred meat in our meals.

But as I grew older, and because of these casual racial epithets thrown my way, I became increasingly sensitive to them. As my awareness of my Japanese identity grew, so did my feelings of perceived estrangement. No one openly teased me anymore for being Japanese—I had endured the worst of that in junior high— but there were other dark occasions when the cultural differences sprang up. My best friend's father would sometimes refer to me as being of the people "who had bombed Pearl Harbor," and my retort to him was "and then you put us in camps for it." I didn't think he was particularly racist at the time; his comments just provoked irritation. When I showed up in a dress that my mother had given me from Japan to wear to a school dance, he complimented me on it and I felt the sincerity of his praise. Yes, I did look and feel pretty in that dress, but no one asked me to dance. Who was going to dance with an Asian girl, after all? There were no other Asian men around to do the asking.

My father continued his valiant efforts in the community to make sure Japanese culture was presented in a positive light to others. One time, I remember a photographer hired for a school textbook was invited to our house to take pictures of our 'typical'

Japanese family eating breakfast in our suburban North American kitchen, and we kids were made to kneel on our chairs in *seiza* position with our legs folded under us, which looked and felt ridiculous, while bringing bowls of rice to our mouths and drinking miso soup. Although all these foods were familiar to me, I rarely ever ate them for breakfast. Neither did I ever kneel on a chair.

How strange it was to be representing a self to the world that I felt was neither true nor accurate to who I really was. But *who* was I?

One place where I found solidarity in this lonely time of adolescent brooding was, oddly enough, the Japanese-language school I went to every Friday night for three hours. The Metro Edmonton Japanese Community School was started in Edmonton in 1977, the year of the 100th anniversary of the first Japanese immigrant's arrival to Canada. While Japanese-Canadian Nisei and Sansei marked this anniversary with festive events all over the country, which in turn awakened their desire to seek Redress for the wrongs done to them during the Second World War, new Japanese immigrants to Edmonton, who were university-educated with a good command of English, decided to start a language school for their children. Our family was involved from the beginning, with even my great-uncle Sanjiro, Auntie Kay's husband, donating a sizable chunk of money for start-up costs. The first school was situated in an elementary school in west Edmonton, which made for a long drive across town for our family from Sherwood Park. In my first years at the school, there were a few teenage girls of junior high age in the class like myself, an older Nisei couple, and some children of Japanese parents who were studying or working temporarily in Edmonton. Remembering the classroom scene now, it appears almost comic: this elegant, middle-aged Nisei couple sitting in desks meant for elementary school kids, the wife in a dress with pearls, the husband in a suit; along with us gangly teenagers in our jeans with our Farah Fawcett feathered hair or our Dorothy Hamill bobs; and the children from Japan looking like they had stepped right out of a *Doraemon* comic book—a Nobita-like boy with bristly cropped hair and glasses wearing a plaid button-down shirt with shorts, a Shizuka-like girl in pigtails and a short pleated skirt with frilly white socks.

Eventually the classes were sorted out more equitably according to the ages of the students and our varying levels of competency. The four of us teenaged girls ended up together in the same class for a number of years. We became fast friends: Lisa (Machiko), Vicki (Kanako), Eiko, and I. We came from different parts of the city—islands of suburbia—where we experienced our own particular versions of cultural isolation and communed in the few hours we had together at the school. Vicki came from St. Albert. Her parents were my godparents. Her father, Yasu, was a biologist, and her mother, Haruko, was a chemistry major and later an instructor of Japanese language at the University of Alberta. Vicki was tall with straight long hair, quiet and shy with, nevertheless, a playful sense of humour. Lisa was also the daughter of scholars: her father was a scientist at the University of Alberta, and her mother, also studying in the sciences, taught Japanese at the university. Lisa was an avid competitive swimmer and reader; we traded stories about swimming and my preferred sport, figure skating. Eiko was the youngest of us; her father was a professor of religion at the university and her mother had been a teacher in Japan. Eiko had a dynamic personality; although she felt the pressure from her parents to achieve—she eventually became a doctor—she pursued acting for a while.

Although the academic side of learning the language was not much fun, I looked forward to going to Japanese school to meet my friends. We complained about having to learn Japanese —we'd hit the *kanji* wall of basic literacy in the language, the point at which learning all the kanji characters becomes prohibitively more difficult without regular practise and exposure. Without such basic mastery of kanji, one could not even read the newspapers in Japan. Although our literacy in the written language was lower than average, our spoken Japanese was much better because we all had Japanese mothers and Japanese was spoken in the home. But, of course, at Japanese school we nattered away in English. We'd meet at recess and share snacks in some nook in the gym or behind the stage where the other kids couldn't see us. The teachers, however, got wind of this and, wanting to enforce the use of Japanese *all* the time, prohibited us from meeting like that. When we finished our last year together at the school—Vicki and I were the first to graduate as we were the oldest—we all went out to a Greek restaurant to celebrate and valiantly tried to conduct our entire meal conversation in Japanese. This got to be harder and harder, especially after a few drinks. Eventually, we ended up in the bathroom—the only place we allowed ourselves to speak in English—laughing and gasping out all the pent-up English words we couldn't speak at our table.

From the beginning, the language school followed the Japanese Mombusho Ministry of Education curriculum for *hoshu-ko,* or overseas schools of learning, which meant we were using the same textbooks Japanese children were using in their schools in Japan. As I grew more sensitive to my cultural identity, I wondered why there couldn't be a more Japanese-Canadian curriculum that would teach us the culture and history of the Japanese in Canada. I wanted something that didn't exist either in my curriculum at my regular high school or now in this Japanese school, which I thought would be more likely to teach me the history of my people in this country, but didn't. The school was run mostly by new immigrants, and, to them, the history of the Japanese Canadians was unknown. Again, I felt like the odd duck in the pond: daughter of a Japanese-Canadian exile-father and a postwar immigrant mother from Osaka. I was not quite part of the old generation of Japanese Canadians in this country, whose members spoke little of the language, but neither was I part of the new postwar urbane class of Japanese immigrants who were well-educated and cosmopolitan in their approach to life.

I was oversensitive and felt differences keenly. Like a cell dividing, I would make a new wall of cells that would separate me from that which once made me whole. And then, perversely, I would yearn for communion with some group that I felt must be out there: whole and just *like* me. If only I could be wholly Sansei, or wholly Japanese, or wholly anything but this mixed-up bag of jumbled identities, I would be fine. And probably not a writer.

Japanese school introduced me not only to the language but also to its literary forms, both high and low. For example, I first learned about haiku in Japanese school, a poetic form that I would return to writing in my later years. I read Japanese folk tales I'd never heard of. In one of our textbooks, there was a folk tale about a childless old couple who scraped all the dead skin off their body while in the bath and made a doll out of it. They breathed into it and, lo, it came to life. They named him, appropriately enough, Akataro, or Dead Skin Boy. My friends and I couldn't believe a Japanese Ministry of Education textbook would contain such a dirty story in it. Here was a Japanese folk tale comfortable with frank expressions about the body that we found hilariously inappropriate. However, in the same textbooks, I would also discover the magical writing of Kenji Miyazawa. Miyazawa was a Taisho-era children's writer and poet who hailed from the northern part of Japan where the climate was harsh but also starkly beautiful; he wrote imaginative tales of a kind that I had never encountered before in English. I would later read his translated poetry and be moved by it also. Miyazawa's writing contained both the wisdom and the innocence of a child; it was a literature that begot wonder, admiration, and gratitude.

Midway through the year in Japanese school, we would stage a *gakugeikai*, a show of stories acted out by the various classes. It was held either in the school gym or in the room rented out in the basement of the downtown Edmonton public library. At first, the plays we performed were the standard Japanese ones performed by Japanese elementary schoolchildren. *"Ooki no kabu"*—"The Giant

Turnip," actually based on a Grimm tale—was one of them. It is the story of an old couple who plant a turnip that grows so big that it becomes impossible to pull out until everyone in the family are all tugging at it together. Since we were an array of school-aged children ranging from eight to fifteen, we made a suitable crew to fill the roles. Little Ken sat hunkered in a bean bag, covered in a white sheet, to recite his lines as the venerable root vegetable, while Vicki and I, with our paste-on ears and crayoned noses, played the family dog and cat. We would stage an annual show for the school, which parents attended and by which they could monitor our progress in the language. By the end of my high school years, however, we decided as a class that we would like to perform our own play for a change, and I offered to write a murder mystery. The play was a fun, collaborative effort, full of stock characters of the kind you'd find in the board game Clue: a Colombo-like detective dressed in a trench coat, a beautiful siren whose useless strongman boyfriend was always fainting, a wealthy old woman with a fortune and dubiously worded will, an absent-minded professor, a lawyer whom I punningly named "Ben Bengoshi" (*bengoshi* is Japanese for "lawyer"), and a cook named Yan Cant (after well-known community TV Chinese-Canadian cook celebrity Yan Can). The play was initially written in English, and then the lines were translated into Japanese. The last time I had tried writing a play was in Grade 6. *Happy Days* was then a popular TV show and the class decided they would stage a skit based on that. However, I was not selected as the writer of the play, as I had expected, but a more popular boy in the class was, who cast me as the Asian cook Arnold, played by Japanese-American actor Pat Morita in the show. Needless to say, I found this typecasting disappointing and the play, on the whole, was nothing like the brilliant piece I had concocted in my head. If anything, writing a play and also being cast in one taught me a few things about the nature of character types *and* stereotypes.

At home, I was exposed to Japanese culture through my grandfather's monthly mailings of the *Asahi Weekly* news magazine. I could not read the densely printed articles about various news topics but I could follow the cartoon strips. There was a strip that featured a typical Japanese businessman, or *sarari man*, which I followed, which then led to an interest in the popular comic series *Sazae-san* by Machiko Hasegawa, about a typical Japanese family all named after seafood (Sazae-san was the main housewife character and was named after an edible shellfish), and another series Hasegawa created called *Ijiwaru Baasan* or "Mean Old Grandma," which I loved reading in digest form.

So I developed an appetite for the visual storytelling of the Japanese through such media as cartoons and manga. Since this literature was considered lowbrow, we were never formally taught to read it, but it was definitely a presence in the Japanese school library and the classroom. The younger students in my Japanese class from Japan would try to sneak in a Doraemon manga to read in class, sandwiching it between the pages of their textbook. I, on the other hand, was increasingly more engaged by Japanese manga for teenage girls, the kind that featured women with inordinately big, glassy eyes wearing natty junior high school uniforms with sailor-like trim and dark pleated miniskirts, who would get embroiled in romantic dilemmas with tall, brooding boys in their dark, stiff-collared, gold-buttoned *seifuku* suits. The trouble was I couldn't read the Japanese in the bubbles, even though I desperately wanted to. I would follow the panels of the comic and would try to interpret what was going on from reading as much of the *hiragana* and *katakana* text that was there. Once I began to learn how to look up kanji in my Nelson's Kanji dictionary, I started translating the manga, one time even writing the translation on white tracing paper, which I would cut into the shape of the conversation bubbles and paste overtop the Japanese. Interestingly, it was also around this time that I would catch a glimpse of Japanese animation on Radio-Canada, French television. Radio-Canada ran such Japanese animation TV programs as *Candy, Candy* and *Heidi*, dubbed in French—shows that ironically featured white-looking characters. Seeing these shows, I'd have the frustrating sense that everything I was interested in culturally had to be mediated through another language. Thus began my lifelong interest in translation.

English, social studies, psychology, sociology, and art became my favourite subjects. These were disciplines in which an exploration and expression of *self*—the self-who-knew-not-what-it-was—could be conducted. When I look back now at the trajectory of my writing career, at what I focused on to obsession, I see that it had to do with the piecing out of my Japanese-Canadian identity. Finding one's identity is a path forged through words, and I was smitten by wordsmithing. I wrote my first published short story in high school and it was about the loss of a *toro*—the stone lantern that one sees in Japanese gardens—by a Japanese-Canadian gardener who had lived through the internment. It was published in the Japanese-Canadian newsletter in Edmonton, the *Moshi Moshi*.

The theme of loss and the symbol of the lantern were already palpable literary inventions in my mind, and I felt the frisson of the creative energy and clarity words can give to an otherwise unexpressed thought or feeling. I became hooked on writing to find out what it could tell me about myself and the culture I felt I was so much in jeopardy of losing. Little was I aware then that this writing impulse existed, too, in my grandfather, but for entirely different reasons. In Japan, he would sit down every day and record something of his life with an eye for detail that was compulsive. He brought into consciousness everything he observed in *words*, and this act, at a very basic level, is what makes a writer, a writer. When he embarked on the writing of his memoir, he had volumes of diaries to consult, which made the memoir all the more compelling to read since he had already recorded so much at first hand. However much my grandfather wrote, though, his writing was not about finding an identity. He was unabashedly Japanese, through and through. I, however, was something else—a hybrid—living in two cultures with different languages, confused about my identity.

To use an Asian-American term bandied around in those days, I was a *banana*: that is, yellow on the outside, white on the inside. By "white," I mean that blank thing all around me that was the "culture" of those days and from which I felt increasingly estranged. To fit into this "white" reality meant being "invisible," and from some perspectives this was advantageous; certainly to "fit in, to assimilate" was the tactic many postwar Japanese Canadians adopted in face of the systemic racism they encountered during the war. But "invisible" was not something *I* wanted to be.

I looked for influences and inspiration to guide my search, but there was nothing in my English or social studies classes that directly addressed the wartime injustices Japanese Canadians faced in Canada, although one of my social studies teachers was aware of it, and it showed up briefly in a National Film Board film called *Propaganda Message,* which the teacher showed to the class; the film made reference to Canadian historical 'skeletons' in the closet. And anything about Japan, the country and its history, was never taught to me directly either, so I sought out contemporary books about Japan that were written by famous historians like Edwin O. Reischauer. In them, the Japanese temperament, cultural traditions, and habits would be explained in encyclopaedic detail. Of course, not having been to the country as an adult, I found it difficult to imagine just how populously dense their cities were with their crowded commuter trains, how intense their educational systems were with their highly competitive entrance exams, and how restricted their lives were by various societal rules and obligations in their family hierarchies and other corporate structures. One particularly revealing book for me on the psychology of the Japanese was Takeo Doi's *Amae no Kozo* (*The Anatomy of Dependence*); its explanation of how the Japanese see the ideal of human relationship as that of between a loving parent and child rang true to me. Whereas independence in adulthood is the ideal in the West, *inter*-dependence in adulthood, in a network of relationships among siblings, peers, and co-workers, would more accurately describe the ideal in Japanese. Here was an interesting interpretation of a self I'd not encountered before: a cell made up *not* of increasing walls of difference that isolated a lonely core, but rather a cell made to attach itself to others in a network of relationships and obligations, a cell whose walls were defined by those other walls it touched around it.

One of those other walls of cells touching my nascent self was visual art. I took a fine art class in high school. Art classes were then divided into "fine art" and "industrial art," and since I was on the university track, I ended up taking the fine art option rather than the more vocational industrial art. Through art class, I learned something fundamental about form. One of the final art projects was to do a painting or drawing of something that would work as a travel poster. Of course, I chose a photo from Japan in a *National Geographic* magazine depicting a rocky outcrop of black stone with white caps smashing against it. I intended, to the best of my ability, to render this scene realistically. Later, I saw a work by an industrial art student who was also given this assignment in her art class. In her rendering of Japan, she had drawn a circular window that looked out onto a garden. The circular window presented a view you would see only in a teahouse in Japan. The lines and shaping of this image were stark and arresting; the image, in fact, was a 'design' and was emblematic rather than realistic. I felt that she had captured a Japanese *aesthetic*, a form, which I had not captured in my more realistic depiction of the Japanese seaside based on a photograph. To me, her creation demonstrated a deeper understanding of an aesthetic I had not really absorbed in my identity-seeking obsession with Japan. This was a significant epiphany. There was a socio-psychological way of looking at one's self through the lens of history *in* a form that was prosaic and realistic, and then there was art—a way of looking at one's self *through* a form that was perhaps unique at one time to a culture, but infinitely transferable to others. The way of art seemed freer and yet restrained at the same time (playing in the garden of forms); the way of socio-psychology seemed unimaginative and yet morally necessary. Exactly which form would work to represent one's true self? I wondered. Which mask would fit the real face behind it? There were obviously other choices out there than the merely prosaic.

If there was a *form* that could do the work of both, a form in which I could be both naked and invisible, different and universal, it was poetry. And poetry, thankfully, found me.

In Margaret Atwood's "Waterstone" lecture about how she became a poet, she describes how a large invisible thumb descended from the sky and pressed down on the top of her head, out of which "a poem formed." This happened to her in her fourth year of high school. She describes her poem as being "quite a gloomy poem [as] the poems of the young usually are," but she spoke of receiving the poem as a gift. "Gift" is a curious word, and how conscious Atwood was in using this word instead of "talent," for example, makes for an important distinction.

Gifts imply a giver and a receiver, and in the Christian worldview, the great giver of gifts is God. As Paul in Corinthians says, "For I would that all men were even as I myself. But every man hath his proper gift of God, one after this manner, and another after that." Although I was losing interest in the church and the ways of the Bible by the time I was in high school, its language about vocation and identity had sunk into the bones of my being.

Similar to Atwood, I, too, received a 'gift' that came from out of nowhere—a dream—that I felt compelled to write as a poem. Yes, it was gloomy. It had blood and other unpleasant things in it, but it was a dream of such significance that I just had to *write* it down. And therein was the gift received and recorded. I showed the poem to my high school English teacher at the time, who read it with some tact and wise sympathy, which I appreciated. I think, just showing her that poem, was also the beginning of my becoming a writer. *I wrote this, I want to show you it. Please read it.*

And so, the poet me emerged in that year of high school—a

larval being of strange hungers, desires, and yearnings who, along with the nascent translator, short story writer, and playwright, sought the written word as a form of expression. By the time I was seventeen, the literary 'stuff' of my being was all there and I felt confident enough to declare it in my school year book, however audacious it sounded. *Sally Ito. Future Ambition: To be a published author.*

Midway through Grade 10 in 1979, my father announced that he would take me to Japan on a trip at Christmas. He had not been back to Japan since 1966, when I was still a toddler. Now that I was in high school and more aware of Dad's family's past in Canada— enough to know, at least, that his family had been the victims of a racist government policy that had forcibly moved them off their Fraser Valley farm and into interior British Columbia during the war—I was curious to find out more of what happened after they left Canada for Japan. Dad never spoke to me directly of what happened; perhaps he assumed I would ingest the facts by osmosis, but it was Auntie Kay who told me everything about their life in Canada before they left. But of what happened afterwards, I had little idea. And there was also my mother's family to visit, a family who'd experienced the war directly, who were the true *enemies* of the nation I lived in and whose perspective I had largely avoided out of shameful denial. To engage with contemporary Japan, with its hip animation and design, was one thing; to engage with its dark wartime past was completely another.

Dad and I were going over the Christmas break for roughly two weeks. I would see all my relatives: grandparents, aunts, uncles, and cousins on both sides, only some of whom I'd already met. It would be exciting, but I was nervous. How would I fare with my spoken Japanese? I used the language at home, but now was the real test: using it in the actual country.

My relatives awaited our arrival with equal parts anticipation and nervousness. Of course, I would be speaking English, they imagined, so how would we communicate? At least I would be with my father, who was completely bilingual. Yoko, my aunt who had visited us in the summer of 1975, was so concerned for my welfare that she bought me a name tag in case I got lost. It was a discreet-looking red ceramic brooch in the shape of a cat with my name and aunt's phone number on it. I had gotten a long, woollen, grey trench coat and a pair of fancy calf-hugging boots that zipped up to the knees, as well as a felt hat, so when I arrived at the airport, I apparently struck my relatives as rather mature and sophisticated for my age.

We visited my mother's family first. The Saitos were *tokai-mono*, or city folk. They were denizens of the brash and boldly mercantile Osaka. Boisterous and talkative, their Osaka dialect fell thick on the ears; it felt oddly comforting to hear, as if my mother's presence were multiplied. My mother's siblings all lived in the Kansai area: her sister, Yoko, and her banker husband lived in Hirakata with their two daughters: Yumi, whom I'd met as a girl the summer she came to Canada, and her older sister, Toshimi. Toshimi was warm and friendly; she quickly linked her arm with mine in sisterly affection as she guided me down the busy train station platforms and down the side streets of Osaka and Kyoto. My Aunt Michiko and her designer husband, Gen, lived in Kusatsu in nearby Shiga Prefecture, with their two younger daughters, Aino and Michino. Michiko had visited Canada when I was a child. At the time, she was in those tender years of her early twenties when her mother had died, but had now become a mother herself, married to a designer of all people, when she had clearly expected to have had an arranged marriage with someone officious and proper, like a doctor.

My mother's only brother, Hidero, and his wife, Yoshiko, lived with their two boys in a new suburban subdivision built into the countryside in a place called Kawanishi Nose-guchi in Hyogo Prefecture. They had recently moved from a more centrally-located neighbourhood in Osaka proper and just had their small yard landscaped by my Ito relatives—my dad's brother, Jimmy, now known as "Toshiyuki" in Japan, ran a nursery in Mie Prefecture—because of the family connection. My grandfather, Toshiro, lived with Hidero and Yoshiko here. He did not look much different from when I had seen him in the past, but my young adult perception of him had changed. I saw him now as a tall, elegant man with a slight stoop whose gait, despite his use of a cane, was smooth and graceful. His room was fastidiously clean and organized; it housed all the accoutrements of his various hobbies: photography, stamp collecting, and reading. The far wall was filled with bookshelves, no doubt containing books like Camus's *L'etranger* and Tolstoy's *War and Peace* and other such literary classics, especially Russian ones, that I would later discover he was fond of reading. Having been sickly when younger, he was very health-conscious, always reporting his various aches and pains to his long-suffering daughter-in-law, Yoshiko. He lifted heavy books to keep in shape. Once I spied him at it: clad only in an undershirt and boxer shorts with two large dictionaries in his hands, he wheezed and grunted as he raised the books from the ground. An avid amateur photographer, he took pains every year to set up a small studio in his room to take his self-portrait, which he expressly told his children was to be used as his funeral photo should he die that year. He was also an atheist; when he died, his body was to be donated to the local hospital for research.

My grandfather felt it was important I be exposed to some traditional Japanese culture on this trip. He made arrangements to take me to a *Noh* concert (very dull) and the *bunraku* puppet theatre (very interesting). He took pictures of me dressed in a kimono. He showed me his photo albums. Recently, he was interested in taking pictures of the *nio*, the guardian statues at nearby temples. Other subjects had been women: he'd hired a nude model to jump into the sea for a shot he had laminated and made into a clock to mount on the wall.

The photo albums were meticulously detailed accounts of his

travels and obsessions. One album was about a trip he'd taken to Indonesia in the seventies. The photos were of a younger him with dark hair, wearing floral print shirts in front of buildings with tropical foliage. I remembered, then, a gift I'd received from him later that he'd sent to my mother, a batik wraparound skirt that I loved wearing. Only later did I realize this trip was for him to revisit the places he'd been when he was posted to Indonesia during the war.

My dad's family in Mie Prefecture was in sharp contrast to my mother's. The Itos were rural people; they lived in the countryside in a farmhouse in a place called Oiwake. Where, in the city, we had often travelled by train, here, we travelled by car. Along the roads I saw paddies and fields with men and women working in them. They wore typical farm garb made out of *kasuri*, indigo print cotton. Sometimes I'd see an old woman by the side of the road, pushing a dusty cart that vaguely resembled an old-style perambulator.

The house in Oiwake where my grandmother Chiyoko lived was wooden and decrepit-looking, a nondescript rectangular box on a squat patch of farmland, dotted with shrubs and small trees. I'm not sure if it was the original dwelling my father's family moved into when they came here from Canada, but it looked like it might have been. The kitchen had a dirt floor, and the bath was still heated by wood. My grandmother lived with her second son, Toshiyuki, who'd assumed the traditional mantle of family responsibility because my father had skipped out of his duties by going back to Canada. Dad was the chonan, or the first-born oldest son, and typically it was the chonan's responsibility to take over the family business or farm or whatever it was the family did for its livelihood. In a pattern that went back to his grandfather, Saichi Ito, a string of first-borns had opted out of their traditional family obligations by skipping town, all of them bound for Canada: Saichi, Shigeru, then Dad. By the time my brother grew up, this pattern would be meaningless in Canada, but in Japan, it continued on with my cousin, Masayuki, who would also skip out on his family obligation to take over the nursery business his father had started in the wake of my father's departure from Japan.

At Toshiyuki's house, we visited with my grandmother, or *Baachan*, as I now referred to her. I could barely remember her from the 1975 summer trip, so it was like seeing her for the first time. Small, slight, and stooped over, Baachan looked like a dishevelled rodent, with a brown wrinkled face framed by loose, unkempt hair that was clearly demarcated by a part that had been dyed (lower half) and grown out (upper half). She wore a winter *hanten*—a Japanese quilted coat—and the cotton trousers known as *mompei*. She was not as talkative as my other living grandparent, my mother's father, Toshiro, but she was aware of what was going on in a quiet way. Mostly she kept to herself, and I heard that her room was a dark, messy den that her daughter-in-law, my aunt, dared not touch. She mucked about the farm; she, too, had a cart that she pushed around everywhere in which she carried her garden tools. Baachan looked after the family dog, a savage white mongrel named Shiro who was kept on a chain far from the house. Shiro had the audacity and stupidity to bite whomever fed him, including my grandmother, who was the only one who risked feeding him.

Our visit occurred during New Year's. Baachan gave me a large sum of money for my New Year's gift—it is customary to give money to children at New Year's—and she also gave me a beautiful lacquered jewellery box to take home. The family hosted a traditional New Year's *mochi-tsuki*, or sticky-rice-making, ritual for us. They made mochi the old-fashioned way, using a large stone mortar and wooden mallet as the pestle. I swung the mallet as hard as I could, trying to pound the mochi. It was a thick, bulbous lump, but I hardly made a dent. Dad, with his man's strength, could whack a crater into the mochi. Baachan stood by, and, between poundings, would slide her hand into the mochi to turn it over. Later, the mochi was taken out of the mortar and made into cakes to be served in *o-zoni,* the New Year's soup. Everything about this ritual delighted me; the family was clearly putting on a show for me and Dad, deeply welcoming us into its midst with customs they had practised in Canada. At home, at New Year's, we made mochi in Uncle Sanjiro's big mechanical mochi maker—Auntie Kay and my mom twisting and rolling off the bits of sticky rice into balls and stuffing them with sweet *anko*, adzuki bean paste.

Since my father had not been to Japan in almost twenty years, this was a big visit for him. He wanted to show the others how successful he'd been in Canada. We made an interminable round of visits to relatives. There was even a term for this kind of visiting: *shinseki mawari*. I hardly knew who we were visiting half the time. Luckily my younger cousin, Toshiko, accompanied me and kept me entertained.

One night we went to a large house in the country. The front entrance was expansive, huger than anything I'd seen before in Japan. And there was, oddly enough, a large plastic structure made out of Lego prominently displayed there. Instead of going in, my younger cousin asked me to go outside with her to explore while the adults visited inside. It was early evening, around twilight. We ran around the sides of the house, and then I caught a glimpse of my cousin poking her finger at a shadowy presence behind a shuttered paper door. "See, that's him," my cousin hissed.

"Who?" I said.

"The guy who built that Lego thing."

I looked again. Beyond the shutters, I could make out a thin man, wearing only underwear, moving spastically about, his fingers curled, wrists bent, his arms twitching by his chest. Why, he has a disability, I thought, the sight disturbing. It was as if I had stumbled on some family shame, some secret I had not been meant to see.

"Who was that?" I asked Dad in the car. He shrugged, said it was his cousin, and didn't elaborate.

Besides Toshiyuki, Dad had two other brothers living in Japan. His youngest brother, Hifumi, whom I'd met the summer of 1975, lived not far down the road from Toshiyuki in a new house built by a major roadway. He and his wife, Sumiko, had three young children. Hifumi had started his own business designing and building warehouse facilities, made out of thick corrugated metal, for farmers in the area to store their machinery and tools. His trademark, he explained, was two white stripes, one thick and one thin, on the blue or red coloured roofs of the buildings he designed. I recognized these stripes on Toshiyuki's outbuilding, and a few more on other outbuildings in the area, so it seemed Hifumi was doing well for himself in this work.

Dad's other brother, Takashi, lived with his family in Nagoya. They lived in a tiny, narrow house out of which he operated a grocery. His small shopfront, which was an extension of the house, abutted the street. There, in the dusky light, I could make out the shape of crates and cartons where vegetables were kept and sold. The entire place struck me as dismal. The family lived in a dark corridor of shop, rooms, and yard. The yard was only a few square metres and very dark; the plants in it were wilted and covered in dust. I don't recall seeing the *furo-ba,* or bathtub, but I remember going with the family to the local bathhouse. It was still customary for a family to go there; many city dwellers in Japan did at the time, having no private baths. After this visit, Dad started talking about helping Takashi, about somehow bringing him back to Canada, giving him a chance at a better life there, as he'd helped his other two younger brothers, Tom and Stan, the ones now living in Calgary, Alberta, and London, Ontario, respectively.

Dad had been doing well in the stock market, particularly with gold; that was the reason why we could take this trip to Japan. Baachan, however, had some choice words for my Dad. "Don't take such risks," she warned him, "or you'll lose even the hairs of your anus."

Dad wanted to show me other aspects of Japanese culture. He made arrangements to visit traditional artisans working in the countryside with someone hosting an Australian on a Rotary student exchange. We met at a house in Nagoya; the Australian was a tall, affable man with curly orange hair. Piling into a vehicle, we rode out in the countryside to visit a papermaker and a small ceramics factory. I was struck by the beauty of the objects made by these craftspeople who diligently practised their arts in ways that had not changed for hundreds of years. The work, detailed and intensive, required dexterity and skill. Here was a traditional Japan I felt instantly attracted to, instantly gratified by. Perhaps in showing me these places, Dad wanted to imbue in me a sense of belonging to a richly complex and beautiful culture. At the ceramics factory, we were allowed to paint our own rice bowls to be glazed later. Dad wrote the names of our family on his rice bowl—Kunitaro John, Akiko, Sally Sachiko, Daniel Narushi, Catherine Naomi—in English and in Japanese.

On our last day at my grandmother's place, I wandered into the big warehouse on the property where my uncle and aunt kept their gardening equipment. They operated a nursery where they grew shrubs and trees for landscapers, so the warehouse was large and cavernous. I was in the building when something caught my eye: a black trunk. On top, in bright white letters by the handle, were painted the words *Chiyoko Ito, Repatriate*.

Repatriate? The word jumped out at me, a discordant jangle. Baachan wasn't a repatriate, I thought, indignant. She was born in Canada. How could she have been classified as that?

I lifted my gaze and saw beyond the open doors of the warehouse. Baachan was pushing her cart down the lane to feed the dog. "Baachan!" I called out, "Baachan!" but she did not hear me. Shiro's shrill yaps filled the air, drowning out my voice.

When would I hear her story? I wondered. *Would she ever tell me?*

After my return to Canada, I wrote a short story about a Japanese-Canadian teenager who brings her grandmother's fan to an art display at her high school; she entrusts its care to a white girlfriend with striking blonde hair and blue eyes, who inadvertently loses the precious fan (it's not clear if she's lost it or taken it) and disappoints the protagonist.

Clearly, what I felt I had been seeking had been found in Japan, but, back in Canada, I could only perceive its loss. In this liminal space, this vacuum between two worlds, grew a desire to go to Japan. After that Grade 10 trip, I became obsessed with the notion of going back there. I was certain I had to go—this time to live rather than visit—to truly find whatever it was I kept sensing I had lost. My mother, seeing the urgency in my desire, arranged for me to stay with her youngest sister, Michiko, and her family in Shiga. Years before that, when I was a child, Michiko had lived with us in Edmonton, attending the University of Alberta for a year. The arrangement was that I, too, would stay a year in Shiga before going to university. And so, in 1982, I left Canada again for Japan.

During the year that I was there, the Japanese government was undergoing a very public campaign to help reunite Japanese children abandoned in Manchuria during the war with their now aging parents living in Japan. Part of the program involved having these now-grown children, who spoke only Chinese, appear on national TV with their testimonies, outlining as best as they could the circumstances of their abandonment. Some had artifacts, like name tags or token objects, left with them; others had only the stories told to them by their adoptive Chinese parents. My aunt and I would watch the TV, transfixed. The segments were short. Appearing one at a time, looking straight at the camera, the subject would speak in Chinese. Overlying the Chinese was the Japanese translator's voice. Poker-faced in the beginning, the men and women would attempt to respond to the off-camera interviewer's questions as succinctly as possible, but often within seconds, their faces would crumple up, tears welling out of their eyes, as they recounted in sobbing spurts the stories of their abandonment. The stories were excruciatingly painful. What struck me most was how these men and women, despite their Chinese clothing, language, and mannerisms, knew without a doubt they were *Japanese*.

I had come to Japan that year on a journey to find something about myself, and now I dimly began to perceive what that something was. My situation was nothing nearly as painful as that of those people who appeared on the TV, but there was something similar in our quests. Was I not here in Japan also as a result of the war and its effects on my own family? I, too, was a descendant of wartime repatriates on both sides—of grandfather Saito from Indonesia on the one hand, and grandfather Ito from Canada, on the other.

There would be no denying that, even two generations later, despite the privilege of growing up in the reasonably tolerant and ostensibly democratic nation of Canada, I was still looking for the motherland. In Japan was embodied the loss of what I felt was missing all these years in my life in Canada, and I would absorb everything I could from its culture and language to shape the writer I wanted to become.

Chapter Six:

The Emperor's Orphans

After fighting with the other gods, the sun goddess Amaterasu fled into a cave. The world was plunged into darkness. Without the sun, crops died off and people began to starve. The gods conspired to lure her out by telling her they had replaced her with another goddess far more beautiful than she was. Then they hung a mirror on a branch. Amaterasu, curious and enraged at the same time, emerged from the cave and was struck by her own brilliant image reflected in the mirror. One of the gods took hold of her, while another blocked the entrance to the cave. Thus restored to the land, Amaterasu's brilliance once more shone in the sky and brought life back to the people.

—Japanese myth

Look in the mirror, Sally. You are Japanese. That is what people see when they look at you. You can't deny what people see. You can't hide from yourself.

—Akiko, my mother

The emperor of Japan is said to be of divine origin, a direct descendant of Amaterasu. In the myth recounted above, the sun goddess desires to be invisible. And why not? The world, after all, is a tiresome place: lonely, terrifying, full of pain and suffering. However, a people cannot do without their god. To be separated from Him or Her, whomever their god might be—the god of the incarnate man, the goddess of the sacred mirror, the god of the inner self—is to be estranged. Orphaned. For a child, being without a god is like being without a parent. For a nation and a people, being without a god is losing one's cultural identity.

The Showa Emperor, or Emperor Hirohito, as he is more commonly known in the West, died on January 7, 1989. He was eighty-seven years old and had reigned over Japan for over sixty years. I happened to be in Japan at the time of his death. The previous fall, I had received a Mombusho graduate research scholarship to attend Waseda University to translate the poetry of Kazuko Shiraishi. I lived in a dorm in Tokyo so I did not see my relatives as frequently as I did when I lived in Kansai at Michiko and Gen's. However, for the winter break, I headed out to visit my Ito relatives in Oiwake.

Baachan was eighty-one and still in good health. A lot had transpired since I had seen her last, including the final departure of her oldest granddaughter, Fumiko, to Canada. Fumiko and I were the same age, both born in 1964. She grew up as a *baachan-ko*, a child raised by her grandmother because her parents were busy working on the land. Raised on her baachan's stories of Canada, a land of mountains larger than the Suzuka range that dominated the view of her house now, and of an ocean from which her great-grandfather fished for salmon so plenteous his boat would almost tip over, Fumiko developed an intense longing for Canada that was unlike anything her other siblings possessed. Paradoxically, I shared with her the same longing for Japan. Since high school, Fumiko had made more than one trip to Canada and was hoping to stay in the country, however she could manage it. As it would turn out, she would apply for citizenship on the basis of her being a Japanese-born child of Canadian exiles—a provision of the Canadian government's Redress settlement.

The settlement was announced on September 22, 1988, the fall I departed for Japan to begin my scholarship. It included a community fund as well as a cash settlement of $22,000 for every man, woman, and child whose family was dispossessed during the war. Clearly, our family was eligible. My father immediately began corresponding with his brothers and his mother on the matter. He would do everything in his power to see that everyone got their share. My visit to Japan was timely in this regard, as I would be around when a delegation of Japanese Canadians and Canadian government officials would come to the country to hold hearings and assess applications by those former exiles who would now be eligible for the settlement. Just before I left for Japan, I had been working for the Vancouver Redress Committee at the Japanese Canadian Citizens Association office in Vancouver, housed in the historic pre-war Japanese-language school on Alexander Street. The announcement had come as a bit of a surprise—on the heels, actually, of the American announcement of apology made by

Ronald Reagan to Japanese Americans—but for us Japanese Canadians, it was the result of a political fight well fought, establishing Japanese Canadians as true citizens of a country which had victimized them as a disenfranchised minority with ties to a country with which Canada was at war. This fight for one's rights as a citizen through democratic and peaceful means became a defining moment for Japanese-Canadian identity.

Part of the process of achieving Redress was the enormous effort of Japanese-Canadian artists, writers, and academics to present their stories compellingly to a largely ignorant and indifferent Canadian public. I felt myself to be part of this small but driven group of community activists. But also, as a writer, I continued cultivating my interest and knowledge of the Japanese language and culture. Deep in my bones, I felt that pursuing the traditional and spiritual legacy that was my heritage was to mine a source of unending inspiration for my work as an artist. This was why I undertook poetry translation as a possible way of getting to Japan for post-graduate work after completing my fine arts degree in creative writing at University of British Columbia in 1986. There was some overlap in these worlds of the prosaic and the poetic, but sometimes they felt distinct from one another.

In Japan, my then eighty-two-year-old grandfather, Toshiro, began writing his memoir, the one that he would eventually give to my mother. The impulse arose when his grandson casually asked him where he was from. The grandson had assumed all long he was from Osaka, but my grandfather replied he was from Tokyo. This led my grandfather to believe it was time to write his life story. So he began a year-long odyssey to complete what would turn out to be a compelling account of his life during the years of the Showa Emperor's long and tumultuous reign.

The emperor's death was preceded by a protracted illness—cancer—during which the nation was kept at bay. The usual year-end festivities and celebrations were muted; instead of the regular New Year's greeting cards, some people sent out cards of apology expressing their regret over the nation's circumstances, which made them unable to celebrate the New Year in the normal fashion.

My Ito kin at Oiwake were largely oblivious to the Japanese media coverage. The house was in holiday mode with my aunt and uncle at their leisure, taking a well-earned rest from their labours on the farm. The death of the emperor came as no surprise to them; months of anticipation had clearly telegraphed the event. The media had ample time to prepare and programming had been made ready for the day well in advance. All channels were focused on the event. The only avenue of escape was to rent a video. Tagging along with my cousin, I went to the local video shop bustling with like-minded consumers, and rented out the American TV series about aliens called *V* to watch over the holiday. When we returned from the store, Baachan had come out from the dusky depths of her room and was perched on a chair, staring hard at the kitchen TV propped up on a shelf on the wall. I sat with her a while in an attempt to fathom her fixation to the screen. It was a scene from a drama. On hearing of the death of the emperor, a man in his fifties recalls the days of his boyhood during the war when he was evacuated to the countryside with schoolchildren his age. One of his classmate's father is a pilot and has surely perished, but the boy is boastful and proud. "Someday I'm going to be just like him!" he declares defiantly and sets out on a voyage of his imagination in a glass fighter plane. The reverie ends, and the man in his fifties wonders what happened to this old schoolmate, the one whose father must surely have died.

Baachan gets up out of her chair. "Sa-ri," she calls me and beckons me into her room. It is dark and hazy inside, full of dust. An unmade bed lies in the corner. From out of a closet, she pulls an old suitcase. Inside are photos: dozens of black and white snapshots.

Shacks lined up in rows against a backdrop of snowy mountains. Scenes from a field day with students clad in white doing calisthenics and acrobatics displays. School group photos of my uncles and their classmates, with their Caucasian teachers. A picture of a funeral with a Buddhist priest in front of the casket. "These are from Lemon Creek," my grandmother croaks out. "You can have them," she says. She gathers the photos and hands them over to me. Unorganized, unsorted—she has kept them all these years in an old suitcase.

Now, she will get back to the TV and watch coverage of the emperor's death, this emperor whose long reign has stretched throughout almost all of my grandparents' lives and whose legacy still haunted my own. My Saito grandfather and my Ito grandmother, I realize, are peers of their divine ruler, and, for them, their lives were as grains of sand swept over by the great tide of events that unfolded under his name in the Second World War.

My grandfather Toshiro's account of the emperor in his memoir was mostly connected to the end of the war. Toshiro was in Indonesia at the time of the emperor's fateful announcement of Japan's defeat and surrender on August 15, 1945.

On that day, the Navy Transport Department ordered my company, Nanyo Warehouse, to gather all its employees in Surabaya in the square inside the base. When I arrived, the place was already filled with people lined up in rows. The men of our company gathered together and fell in with them. Although we'd heard on the short-wave radio that Japan had surrendered, we wondered what was going to happen to us. An officer said we would hear a speech from the emperor on the radio. He asked us to listen with the utmost respect, indicating how we should straighten up our bodies. Instead, I looked at my watch.

Suddenly, a big crackling noise came from the speakers. I could hear a voice, but couldn't recognize it as speaking a language. It was the emperor, probably saying something apologetic from his heart, and in spite of myself, my eyes grew wet with tears. The thought of him transported me back to a time when I was a junior high school student. I'd seen the young prince as an officer then in front of the Imperial Palace. How regal he looked, and yet how vulnerable. This was before he had become emperor. Hearing his voice now reminded me of that long-ago memory. And now all of it— his ascension to the throne, the expansion of his empire—had all come to this terrible end. Japan had lost the war. My tears were for the nation.

By this time, back home in Japan, my mother and her family had evacuated to the mountainous terrain in Hyogo Prefecture behind Osaka to a town called Nose. Unlike other children who were sent to rural temples while their parents remained in the city, my mother's family evacuated together. After a harrowing nighttime air raid by American bombers in Osaka, during which my grandmother tried escaping to her brother's place—she was turned away because there were too many others taking refuge there—she decided to evacuate the family into the countryside on her own. A ramshackle house made of wood and scrap metal, perched on a steep hillside, was procured from a nearby farmer, paid for by my mother's father. And so it was that my grandmother, who had been a pampered urbane woman with a good education, found herself alone and saddled with the care of three young children in a mountainous village at a considerable remove from the city. In the mountains, the weather was cooler; so cool, in fact, that the area specialized in making *kanten*, or agar, which requires sub-zero temperatures in its production.

For children coming from the cities, life in the country was rough and brutish. There was bullying. My uncle was forced by some older boys to drink the muddy and bacteria-laden silt waters of the rice paddies; it made him sick. My mother took to vehemently defending him against his tormentors and thus developed a reputation among the other schoolchildren as a girl not to be trifled with.

Food was rationed and rice was scarce. Luxury items like kimonos were bartered for a sack of barley or a bag of potatoes. When I think of the silks my genteel and well-heeled grandmother might have owned at the time, I mourn their loss. Impractically beautiful, they had an allure of their own, enough to make a farmer want to trade food for them. When would a farmer ever wear such a thing? Here was a luxury so beautiful and yet so useless, it could charm someone so completely as to abandon common sense. And all for what? A couple of meals' worth. *My kingdom for a horse.* My kimono for a bag of potatoes.

If it wasn't for this wartime move into the mountains, Mother and her siblings would not have learned how to forage in spring. There was plenty to eat if you knew what to look for and how to prepare it. Early spring—March and April—brought forth numerous succulent edibles like the tender, three-leaved *mitsuba*, the stalks of the hairy *udo*, or the celery-like *fuki*. The new leaves of the prickly ash shrub known as *kinome* and its peppercorn-like fruit—*sansho*—made a piquant addition to a bowl of rice. The most anticipated edible of the season was the meaty *takenoko*, or bamboo shoot, that stuck up out of the ground like a rocket canister with its hairy, pointed husk. You needed a good sharp hoe to uproot these shoots, and a sturdy basket or bucket to carry them home. Some of these *sansai*, or spring greens, were familiar to the

Japanese in the Canadian mountains and, ironically, were being harvested by internees slightly later on in the season, as I would recall Auntie Kay telling me.

For protein and minerals, Mom ate the imperially recommended items printed in newspapers at the time to help the starving populace. She'd eaten grasshoppers, for instance, as well as the tiny freshwater crabs—*zenigani*, my mother called them—that could be collected in mountain streams. The children would take them home, boil them, and eat them, shell and all, crunching them like crackers.

The coming of spring must have meant much to the Japanese then; a return of hope, a chance to somehow survive and beat the odds. Foraging was now an eagerly anticipated event by a population starved by the machination of their country at war. It's ironic, insofar as early spring has always struck me as a violent season: the plants that emerge from the leafy detritus of the past are pointy tips, spears, and shoots. They must puncture through layers of the dead growth above them and proclaim their right to life in aggressive, vibrant greens. To a starving and exhausted population, these bullets of the season produced by nature's munitions factory filled their bellies after years of the people having given every ounce of energy to a war they had lost.

Many years later, at my wedding banquet, my uncle gave a speech on the fortitude of my mother in those years: "We knew Akiko would end up abroad because she always said she'd go to foreign lands when she was a girl. One spring, just after the war ended, we were out foraging in the woods, crawling on our hands and knees, when all of a sudden, Akiko shot up from the ground and said in a loud voice, 'I'm going to Paris someday, just you watch me!'"

Japan's defeat meant the return of its citizens from abroad. Around 6.5 million Japanese were spread all over Asia, Siberia, and the

Pacific in the wake of the country's surrender. Most of these Japanese, including both my Saito and Ito grandfathers, *wanted* to return home. For them, *repatriate* was an accurate term. It reflected an inner reality: the desire to return home as quickly as possible to be reunited with loved ones.

My grandfather Toshiro, who was in Indonesia at war's end, and his colleagues at the Nanyo Warehouse Company retreated with other Japanese navy non-combatant employees to a place called Puchong in a cool, mountainous area of Malang in the interior. He stayed there for several months until he and the others were shipped out to Singapore in May 1946. There, he was housed in a repatriation centre with other non-combatant repatriates until June. From this centre, he would board one of many American transport ships that were used to bring Japanese from all corners of the world back to their home country. In his memoir, he writes of his return in 1946:

> The time came for our departure on June 10. Orders arrived to board the ship. All the Nanyo employees could board but we had to fill out application forms. I found out why later. The ship we were on was an American navy transport called the *Liberty*. Before that, the Allies used Japanese vessels to repatriate their citizens and so there was no need for forms. Ships like the *Liberty* were no-frills army transports. However, we didn't care; we were just so happy to be going home, we didn't complain. Not only that, but when we passed through the Basu Strait where the barometric pressure was low and caused the ship to toss so badly that one could hardly walk, the people who normally would have gotten seasick at such a time were nonetheless cheerfully carrying out their duties as kitchen

help, producing fine meals at a time when they might otherwise be too nauseous to work.

The ship arrived at Ohtake Harbour in Hiroshima. When we disembarked, we were met by British soldiers. First, they sprinkled white powder all over us with an air pressure hose, even putting it in our underwear. It was shocking and humiliating to be treated like this. Later, I found out the powder was DDT. They took all my military scrip and confiscated my bank account book from Java, and gave me instead a brand new 1,000 yen bill. Then I went out.

A telegram had been sent already to company headquarters about our presence on the ship so someone had been sent to meet us. That person told us the fate of our families and homes while we were away. Some were given good news about their families' situations and, of course, they were overjoyed. But others received terrible news of family members perishing in bombings or homes being destroyed, and they wept with grief. Most of us had no clue as to what had been going on in the country because we'd been away so long. People were experiencing all kinds of emotions, myself included. In the midst of all this exchange of news, I was told my family had evacuated to the mountains outside of Osaka.

For people to return to their homes—east and west—we were given free tickets for the train.

In Hiroshima, the term used at the time for the atomic bomb was the "Pikadon." ["Pikadon" is an onomatopoeic word describing the flash of the bomb—PIKA—and the tremendous

booming sound—DON—that came right after.]
When our train sluggishly passed Hiroshima station, I couldn't believe the sight that greeted
my eyes. The city as I remembered it had completely vanished. In its place was a burnt-out
field stretching out for miles. Little remnants of
buildings poked up here and there; the people walking around still seemed in a daze even
though it had been a year already since the
bombing. The place looked unreal, as if time
stood still

When I arrived in Osaka, I got off the train
and, from the upraised station, could look down
at the city below. It, too, had been devastated
from the bombings. Expanses of it were burnt
out with charred remnants of buildings sticking
upright from the ground like blackened stumps.
But when I looked down at the people mill-
ing about in the typical hustle-and-bustle way
of Osakans, I felt somewhat cheered. Osaka,
with its vibrant and robust merchant sensibility,
would surely get back on its feet. The majestic Hankyu Building stood tall as ever, and the
trains were all in operation, whistling in and out
of the station, regular as clockwork, the way it
always had been.

With my rucksack on my back, gaiters on my
legs, and my war uniform cap on, I looked con-
spicuous. People would stop by me, asking the
same things: "Where did you come from?" or
"Where are you going?" I said I'd just returned
from Indonesia and wanted to go home to
Higashi Nose village and that I was going to
take the Nose train. Someone told me I should

take a bus from Ikeda to Higashi Nose as the train didn't go that far into the mountains. I was surprised to hear that, but the fellow was right. I could get to the village only by bus. It headed out of the city and wound its way into the mountains through a narrow valley studded with old farmhouses of the kind you read about in folk tales. So this is how far the family had evacuated! I thought they must be living like country bumpkins.

Once I stepped out of the bus at the little terminal, I began walking in the direction I assumed where the home was located. There were two or three elementary school kids skipping along nearby. I thought Akiko, my daughter, would be about the same age as these children and might even go to the same school so I asked them, "Do you know Akiko Saito?" As soon as they heard my question, they ran off right away without even bothering to give me a reply! I kept trudging along and then all of a sudden from a bend in the road, I could see Akiko come running as fast as her little legs could carry her, her arms flung out as she cried, "Daddy, Daddy!" I squatted down at once and held out my arms. She ran into them and clung to me, sobbing. Probably those other children had told her they had seen me coming. Holding my daughter's quivering body in my arms, I, too, began to cry in spite of myself. For four long years, little Akiko had been waiting and yearning for the day she would see me again.

When the delegation of the National Association of Japanese Canadians and Canadian government officials came to Japan in August 1989 to seek out those exiles eligible for Redress, I was able to accompany my uncles and my grandmother to Hikone in Shiga, where one of the hearings was to take place. Dad had already helped with the initial preparation of the paperwork and so we went to the meeting together, quite hopeful.

During that car ride, I began to piece together what happened to my father's family in Japan. I had a slightly better knowledge now of the wider context of the impact during the war on Japanese Canadians in Canada because of my work on Redress, but I was still unfamiliar with what happened to my family after they came to Japan.

At roughly the same time my grandfather set out on his return voyage as a repatriate to Japan from Singapore, the first of the American transports, the SS *Marine Angel,* shipped out of Vancouver, bound for the port of Kurihama, Japan. The passengers on this boat were also described as "repatriates," but unlike my grandfather, these were not necessarily Japanese Nationals yearning for home. Rather, some of them were Canadians of Japanese descent who had never set foot in Japan or, as in my father's mother's case, had chosen out of duress and despair to go to Japan. Shabbily treated in Canada, they left like refugees from it.

Ironically, Canada is said to have received almost 165,000 refugees from Europe during the immediate postwar period, while expelling nearly 4,000 of its own citizens at the same time. At war's end, interned Japanese Canadians were given two choices by the governing authorities: resettle east of the Rockies or go to Japan. By selling their properties and means to their livelihoods on the west coast and putting a ban on their return there, the government intended to disperse Japanese Canadians. Those who chose to stay were felt to be 'loyal and assimilable.' Those who did not want to stay were considered 'disloyal and unassimilable.' In the eyes of the government, there could be no hope for the latter but to send them to the country of their racial origin. In an oddly disjunctive manner, these so-called repatriates would become part of a massive effort that saw over five million Japanese repatriated to Japan's shores from all corners of its former empire. But these repatriates were different. Fully two-thirds of the 4,000 who went to Japan were Canadian-born children. Technically, many were not repatriates but exiles. And, in keeping with their birthright, many would return to Canada, like my dad.

The process that led to repatriation of Japanese Canadians is manifold and complex. Politically, the program for dispersal was launched in the spring of 1945. With the war seemingly close to its end, a 'solution' had to be found for the Japanese Canadians languishing in the camps. Notices began to appear that offered the two choices of resettling or going to Japan. The options were presented in a strikingly deceptive manner. For example, for those wanting to repatriate, the notice read that "free passage would be guaranteed by the Canadian government, including free transportation of their personal property." For those wanting to remain, the wording read more ominously that "failure to accept employment east of the Rockies may be regarded at a later date as lack of co-operation with the Canadian Government in carrying out the policy of dispersal." Nowhere in the policy were Japanese Canadians offered the chance to return to the coast, despite the fact that by this time the United States had revoked the west coast exclusion orders for Japanese Americans because a Japanese attack was no longer a substantial possibility.

Of course, when these options were presented to my grandparents, my dad was a boy.

Neither he nor his brothers has any recollection of the decision. But Auntie Kay told me about the acrimony between my grandparents, Chiyoko and Shigeru, over the matter. Chiyoko did not want to go; Shigeru, however, did. Everyone in the immediate Ito family counselled against Shigeru's desire to go. However, Shigeru remained undeterred. He signed the repatriation papers. Chiyoko held back. As a Canadian citizen, signing would mean revoking her citizenship. This was serious: if she signed, there would be no going back.

In August, two atomic bombs were dropped on Hiroshima and Nagasaki. On September 2, Japan officially surrendered. At this time, many who had opted for repatriation wanted to change their minds. Labour Minister Mitchell announced that any Canadian-born or naturalized citizen who submitted a request for the cancellation of their repatriation order by the surrender date would be permitted to stay. Cancellation of requests by Japanese Nationals, however, would not be considered.

Shigeru's course was set. Chiyoko's, however, remained in limbo. During that uncertain summer month of 1945, she threatened not to sign. But by September, she could see no recourse but to comply with her husband's wishes. With five children, she could neither take them to southern Alberta where her parents were, nor send them with her husband to grow up without their mother in Japan. In anguish and chagrin, my grandmother signed the repatriation papers. She would never live in Canada again.

Five ships carrying repatriates departed Vancouver from May through August of 1946. My father's family's ship, the *General Meigs*, left in August. The ship docked at Kurihama, one of ten designated ports of repatriation.

Despite living in harsh conditions in the interior camps of British Columbia, the Itos were overwhelmed at the sight of the devastated country. It was a completely different place from what Shigeru had remembered decades earlier. Gloom and misery pervaded the air as the Canadians milled among the many other repatriates coming through the port. There was no special reception for them; they were but a drop in the bucket of thousands of repatriates arriving daily back into the country. At the repatriation centre, the boys were given *dango-jiru* to eat, a gruel made of bug-infested millet. From Kurihama, the family proceeded by train to the honke, or main family house, in Sobue in Aichi Prefecture, the house that Saichi had abandoned earlier as the chonan. The house had passed onto the care of Saichi's brother, Sentaro, who had eleven children, of whom Shigeru was the oldest. Shigeru, who should have inherited the post, but did not, was forced by his parents into marriage with his cousin Chiyoko in Canada for reasons that would not become clear until his death.

It was to this house in Sobue that Shigeru, with his five children, returned. There, he hoped in some vague way to be greeted and welcomed by his family, whom he had not corresponded with for years and to whom his children were complete strangers. In a way, it was a return of the prodigal, except that now, there was no loving father to greet him, for he had died. Only his bitter mother, who had many other sons to worry about than the one who had left for Canada, remained in the house. For Chiyoko, however, returning to the honke was reliving a nightmare. This was the very house she had been left in years ago when she was a girl. To return to it empty-handed with five young mouths to feed, and made to impose on an already constrained host—her widowed mother-in-law, who had picked on her when Chiyoko was younger, and her brother-in-law, Kaoru, and his wife—was more than she could bear. Chiyoko cried every day. What made things worse was the discovery she was now pregnant with a sixth child.

War-ravaged Japan felt no love towards its returnees. Even my Saito grandfather, who felt happy on his return to his beloved Osaka after his years away in Indonesia, got the cold shoulder from his wife. After describing his tearful reunion with my mother, he writes in his memoir:

> Holding my daughter in my arms, I walked towards home. Soon, from a house right by the street, my wife, Kiyoko, emerged and was bidding farewell to the residents. She knew about my arrival because a telegram had been sent ahead. She acknowledged me with a "Oh hello,

you're back"—quite unlike Akiko's boisterous
welcome—and walked briskly on ahead of me.
I was taken aback by her indifferent reception,
and found myself questioning her cold attitude.

Historian John Dower speaks of postwar Japan as a harsh,
inhospitable place for anyone who did not fall into a proper social
category. Indeed, some of the country's most pathetic war victims—disabled veterans, atomic bomb survivors, homeless widows, orphans—became instant outcasts. Predictably, repatriates
from Canada were not considered Japanese. They were referred
to as *gaijin*, or "foreigners," or, worse, as "Yankees." With resources
scarce, the country considered them an unwelcome burden.

I'm sure it was then that my twelve-year-old father resolved to
return to Canada.

Unable to take over the family estate since his brother Kaoru
was now running the place, Shigeru moved his family to land in
Oiwake, Mie Prefecture. An investment plot had been purchased
earlier by his younger brother Noboru, and was being cultivated
by another younger brother, Minoru, who had just received his
call-up papers when the war ended. During the war, this part of
Mie had been converted into an airstrip. Afterwards, it was dismantled and the property taken over by the *kaitakudan*, the Colo-
nists Organization. As part of the new land reform scheme enacted
by the Occupation authorities, the kaitakudan parcelled out this
land to returnees from Manchuria. Shigeru bought into this land,
the only non-Manchurian repatriate, so that he could farm alongside his younger brother.

Because the land had been an airstrip, there was little topsoil.
The ground was hardened clay. Cultivating it was back-breaking
work. Anything that could be found was used as fertilizer: grass,
compost, night soil. Hogs were raised in the early years for their
manure, fed on the hardy *susuki* grass that grew on the clay. Food
was scarce; the family lived on a subsistence level. Meals consisted

of a large communal pot of vegetable stew, which the boys had to fight over to serve themselves. The land was unsuitable for planting rice so sweet potatoes became the dominant crop. My uncle Stan remembers going to school and seeing the village children with rice in their lunches. The children of the kaitakudan had no such luxury. "We used to go past the village houses, and they had trees full of persimmons. We would steal them, we were so hungry," Stan would say later. Because of food shortages, vegetable thievery was common. In winter, the boys ate sweet potato dumplings made from tubers that were dried and ground into a powder, which was later mixed with water to form the doughy balls.

The boys went to the local school. On the first day, my father strode into the building, brothers in tow, with his shoes on. The boys clattered onto the smooth wooden floors, unaware they were breaching school rules by not removing their footwear. At first, they huddled together in the schoolyard, speaking English, but eventually they would blend in with the others, Japanese slowly overtaking the English until the latter would become nothing but a vestigial memory. This was true for the boys except for my father, who made every effort to maintain his English.

The privation the Itos suffered in those postwar years was no different from that suffered by many Japanese families of the time; indeed, my mother's family underwent worse, having survived the aerial bombardment of the cities. But for my father's generation of repatriates—helpless children, for the most part—the damage was psychological. Their parents had known a better life, and had chosen the worst of the alternatives. There would be consequences.

In 1954, Shigeru died from skin cancer. He was forty-nine. By this time, all the brothers, with the exception of Stan and the youngest, Hifumi, had finished or were close to finishing junior high school, which was considered a terminating point for the boys' education. If they were to go further, they would have to do so at their own expense and time. It was while in junior high that my father began translating for the port authority in nearby

Yokkaichi; he then transferred to the quarantine department of the same authority in Nagoya, where he worked to finish his high school at night. His dedication to the study of both languages in those years made him completely bilingual. There was not a trace of an accent in either his spoken English or Japanese; he could also read and write both. In this way, he became, oddly, a master of disguise, appearing Japanese to the Japanese, and English-speaking Canadian to the Canadian.

If there was a moment's hesitation in my father's resolve to return to Canada, it was at the time of his father's death. He could inherit the land he and his brothers had worked so hard to cultivate, if he so wished. As chonan, he had the right. But by then, the land was alien to him. He had bigger dreams than to till a patch of hardened clay in a country shaky on its legs after losing a war. Canada was where he was from, and where he longed to return. Life was better there. This was a fact no one in postwar Japan could deny.

My father gave over his portion of the land to his second-oldest brother, Jimmy, now called Toshiyuki, who reluctantly took over the family farm although he, too, longed to return to Canada. Soon thereafter, my father was on a ship sailing towards Vancouver. Because he had been an underage dependent of a repatriate, he had not lost his status as a Canadian and was therefore able to return as long as there was a sponsoring relative. This relative was his uncle Jack in southern Alberta, to whose farm my father went immediately. There, he was reunited with his aged grandfather, Saichi, and grandmother, Ei, whom he had not seen since the clan's forced break-up in 1942.

Although my father had abandoned his post as chonan, the responsibility he felt as the oldest never left him. As soon as he arrived in Canada, he hoped to bring all his brothers back as well as his mother. But in the end, only two brothers would come: Stan and Tom. They arrived in 1958 when my father was at the Provincial Institute of Technology and Art, now called Southern Alberta Institute of Technology, or SAIT, in Calgary, training to be a radio operator. A group of my father's friends from school jumped into a car and drove to Vancouver to pick the brothers up. From then on, my father would see to the needs of these brothers until they gained a foothold in the country.

It was in Calgary that my father ran into an old boyhood acquaintance from Lemon Creek, George Miyagawa. George's parents were also repatriates. George had returned to Canada from Shiga Prefecture with his Japanese wife, Keiko, and was now working in the Canadian army. In George and Keiko, my father saw the model of a marriage he wished to emulate. He, too, wanted a Japanese wife. Keiko, who is my mother's cousin, agreed to set my father up with someone she used to work with at the Takashimaya department store, which had a reputation for hiring beautiful women as its store clerks.

Here's how my grandfather explained what happened with this arrangement in his memoir:

> Actually to back up a little, John was not going to marry Akiko at first. Although it may sound funny to say this, but their meeting struck me as fatefully accidental in the way humans meet and interact. The woman my niece, Keiko Miyagawa, had intended to introduce to John was a friend of hers named Keiko Kohno. Keiko Miyagawa recommended to John that he go to Japan to meet Keiko Kohno, and Keiko Miyagawa told Keiko Kohno this as well. Just then, hearing of this talk from John, his friend from radio school, the East German refugee Hans Frueh became interested in the 'convenient' customs of Japanese marriage arranging, and wanted to explore more and get a taste of this unknown country and culture. Hans decided to visit Japan. "If you're going," said

John, "then please meet with this Keiko Kohno
and tell me what you think of her." John made
this remark light-heartedly. What a mistake!
Hans fell in love with Keiko at first sight, and
quickly married her in Japan.

Because of this unexpected twist of events, Keiko Miyagawa
then quickly set about arranging something between my father
and her cousin—my mother—Akiko Saito of Osaka. After a brief
exchange of letters and photographs, Mom and Dad were married in 1962 in Japan. My father returned to Canada soon after
the wedding to take a job as a radio operator with the federal government in Fort Wrigley, Northwest Territories. My mother would
arrive soon thereafter to her first home in the country: an outpost
of five houses on the Mackenzie River. I was born two years later in
1964 in Taber, where Mother had been flown down to be with the
family who had sponsored her husband's return to Canada, Jack
and Molly Ito of Cranford, Alberta.

We arrived in Shiga safely and filed our applications for the Redress
payments there. There was a slight glitch, however, with Hifumi.
Having been born in Japan after their arrival there, this meant
he would be ineligible for payment. Still, everyone else living in
Dad's family would be eligible: Chiyoko, Jack, and Kay (Saichi and
Ei's three Canadian-born children), and Dad, Toshiyuki (James),
Takashi (George), Stan, and Tom.

While in Shiga, I talked with some friends I had made while
working on Redress in Vancouver who were part of the visiting
delegation, and heard the stories of other exiled Japanese-Canadian families, some of whose circumstances were worse than my
family's. Many Japanese Canadians, for example, came from Hiroshima Prefecture, the site of the atomic bombing, and lost family
members in the explosion. Joy Kogawa's book *Obasan* explores the

fictional tragedy of such a family from Nagasaki. There were others, much like the character of Naomi's mother in *Obasan*, who were stuck in Japan during the war, unable to return to Canada to their parents or their children. I realized my grandmother's wish to keep her family together was the compromise she made in giving up her citizenship rights to the country of her birth.

Looking at her in the car, I felt something of the sense of the words my grandfather Toshiro wrote of her in his travel diary from that long-ago summer trip in 1975:

> I had really gotten to know John's mother, having spent almost half a month with her on this trip to Canada. She had been widowed early and had to raise six boys on her own, and she was still working on the family farm. She had wrinkles on her face that showed her experiences of hardship in life. She had a strong spirit that had endured much—rain or shine. She did not talk much but observed quietly and sharply the things going on around her; sometimes she would smile or laugh but there was always something sharp, almost glinting in her look. I looked at John's mother and thought she was a great woman.

Near the end of my research scholarship term in the spring of 1990, my mother decided she wanted to visit Japan with Auntie Kay while I was still there. My grandfather records why in the final few pages of his memoir:

> I was hoping to finish this memoir by my eighty-third birthday on April 19. Considering my health, I did not feel that I would live much longer so I called Akiko to visit me. I wanted to see her before I died and talk about various things with her. I made an international phone call to her

and asked her if she would come, and she said okay. It turned out, however, that Akiko had many other reasons to come to Japan other than to just see me. First of all, she was going to take her husband John's aunt, Auntie Kay, to see Kay's sister, Chiyoko, at the Ito house in Oiwake. And the plan was that she would take Chiyoko back with her to Canada with Auntie Kay. That was the first main reason for a visit. She also wanted to take Auntie Kay to the home-town of Kay's late husband, Sanjiro, who was originally from Oita, Kyushu, and let her meet with his relatives. Another reason she wanted to visit was to see her daughter, Sally, who was in the graduate program at Waseda University in Tokyo.

Dad would stay at home. Although he'd had a heart attack five years earlier that had landed him in hospital, he had recovered significantly enough by moderating his diet and exercising that my mother felt comfortable leaving him for a spell.

Mom and Auntie Kay arrived rather circuitously through taking a Korean Airlines flight that had unceremoniously landed them in Tokyo from Seoul at two o'clock in the morning because of a booking error. I remember being called to the front desk at the dorm, where I saw my mother and aunt, looking tired and fatigued from their travels. In particular, my mother was concerned about some vacuum-packed beef she had brought as gifts for the family that had not made it with her as luggage when she arrived in Tokyo.

It was an inauspicious start to a trip that would end abruptly. My mother had a full itinerary of people she wanted to see and places she wanted to go. I accompanied them for some of the journey, going to Kyushu for the first time to visit Auntie Kay's in-laws there, and going to Oiwake to see my grandmother with them. It was in Oiwake that we heard the news. We had gone out the day before when Auntie Kay had misplaced her camera somewhere, and so we went out looking for it. On our return to the house, someone came running out saying they'd received a phone call with the news that Dad had died of a heart attack in Edmonton. He had gone for a jog by himself when he collapsed about a block away from the house. He did not have his nitro pills on him. A teenage boy found him on the street, and an ambulance was called. He died enroute to the University Hospital in Edmonton.

Just the night before, lying in our futons laid out side by side in the tatamied room not far from the butsudan in my uncle Toshi-yuki's house, my mother confided to me that she had a notion that she and Auntie Kay were fated to be widows together in Canada. Still, the death was a shock. Dad was only fifty-five years old.

I can remember the weeping of my grandmother, Chiyoko, the whimpers emanating from her tiny body. *Un ga warui.* She'd always told me "Fate is bad" and now, of all the indignities she had suffered, seeing her oldest son die before her was the worst. The family quickly drew together, deciding that all the Ito brothers in Japan, along with Chiyoko and the rest of us, would fly immediately to Canada for Dad's funeral. As I was at the end of my scholarship term in Tokyo, I went back up to Tokyo to collect my things and found a letter from Dad. The tone was cheerful, but also wistful. In it, he referred to what he'd been doing for the family for Redress; all the paperwork had been completed and now all there was to do was wait. He remarked briefly on his health, probably to reassure me. I held that letter in my hands, standing in the hallway of my dorm, and wept.

All that occurred afterwards was a blur, but my grandfather recorded it faithfully in his memoir which he was just finishing up the spring of 1990, allowing me his perspective on the event:

> On the morning of April 21st, Michiko, crying on
> the phone, told me she'd just received a call

from Akiko's daughter, Cathy, telling her that John had died suddenly. On hearing this, I was in shock and at a loss for words. He had almost died several years ago from a heart attack. Knowing that this news must have certainly reached Akiko in Oiwake by now, I felt just terrible at the irony of fate that had me invite Akiko to visit so she could see me while I was still alive only to have her not be there for her husband's death in Canada. In the ensuing days, through the strength of her faith and her strong character, she handled the matters of her return to Canada and other arrangements with such calm reserve that I was impressed and very proud of her.

When Mom and I finally arrived home in Sherwood Park with all our relatives, I walked into Dad's office. There, on his desk, unopened, lay a beige envelope from the Government of Canada. It was his cheque for Redress. Had he laid it there, I wondered, before he took that fateful jog around the block?

Dad's funeral would be the only time all his brothers and his mother would be in the same room in the country of their birth since the end of the war. I remember a photo taken of all of my uncles—Toshiyuki, Takashi, Tom, Stan, and Hifumi—along with my grandmother, Chiyoko, Auntie Kay, and Uncle Jack and Aunt Molly—who had come up from Cranford—gathered together in the family living room. Moments before, Mom knelt in the traditional seiza manner on the plush green carpet of the living room, placing her hands in front of her, and bowed so deeply her forehead almost touched the ground. She thanked everyone for coming and for all they had done to make her and my father's prosperous and comfortable life in Canada possible.

When I looked at the embalmed, waxen corpse of my father

in a suit in the casket at the funeral home, my first feeling was of absence. *That's not Dad*, I thought. *Where is he?*

In our evangelical Christian home, the final destination after death was heaven, but heaven was contingent on accepting Jesus Christ as one's own personal saviour. Dad had not done this, not in any public way, at least, so in my vestigial anxiety left by my Christian upbringing, I wondered if he was there or not. Of course, there was also hell, but, thankfully, none of the Christians around us were bringing up that possibility. Still, I remembered that one of my mother's friends had tried to evangelize to Dad in the hospital when he had his first heart attack, or so I heard, second hand. I wondered: how does one even talk of the gospel to a man who lived obligingly with its constant presence in the lives of his wife and children? Dad had a passing familiarity with Jesus but not of that childish kind in which one's whole heart can be made to sing, with utmost confidence, "Jesus Loves Me, this I know, for the Bible tells me so."

Whom did Dad have, I wondered, *instead of Jesus? Whom was he looking forward to seeing in that land of death called Heaven?*

I guess what I was ultimately asking myself was, *Whom did he really love?*

A few weeks after Dad died, Mom had a dream. Dad came to her in radiant garb, arrayed in gold jewellery, and asked her how she was doing. She told him she was fine. There was some life insurance money and the Redress cheque was used to pay off the remaining mortgage, so materially, she was looked after. She told him he needn't worry about her. Mom woke up from that dream reassured.

It was then I knew Dad *loved* Mom and, even in his great absence, found a way to tell her so.

When Dad died, at the cusp of Redress, it was like he disappeared into a hole. From then on, the very god of my Canadian identity disappeared, and I, for many years, struggled to coax the memory of him out of myself to find in it the chipped and shattered bits of my own particular form of Canadian identity. Many years later, in an article for the *Globe and Mail*, I wrote on my father's family's history, this was the conclusion I came to about Dad:

> I believe one's cultural identity is forged in the furnace of circumstance. And my father's circumstance was extraordinary in every way.
>
> Dad spent the early part of his childhood in Canada, unaware of the racist forces that conspired against him and his community; these forces would go on to expel him from the only home he had ever known. The next part of his life would be spent in Japan when the country was at its most wretched and inhospitable. That Dad would spend his adolescence dreaming of Canada was understandable. When he returned, it must have felt like a homecoming. But one doesn't spend a decade of one's childhood in one country and a decade in another without both having an effect on who one becomes in the end.
>
> The irony of the repatriation policy of the federal government was that it made people like my father both loyal and unassimilable. Dad was as determined a Canadian as he was Japanese; all his life, he played the role of a bridge between two worlds. His legacy to us was the sheer agility he displayed in spanning two cultures in an existence that was ever conscious of the forces of fate that had shaped it.

CHAPTER SEVEN:

SAICHI'S LAND

Gravestones

Behind the cemetery,
A fence is going up.

The gravestones will no longer
be able to look out to sea

nor see their children,
and their children's children
get on and off the boats
that are coming and going.

There's a fence going up
along the seaside path.

We boys will no longer
be able to see the gravestones,

especially our favorite,
the one we always look at, passing by
the smallest, round one.

—Misuzu Kaneko

On our arrival in Japan in the spring of 2007, I took our family to visit the graves of their ancestors: my grandparents and my children's great-grandparents.

My maternal grandparents, Toshiro and Kiyoko Saito, were interred in Kyoto, in Higashi Ohtani cemetery, the temple of which served as a mortuary for abbots of the nearby Higashi Honganji Temple, the headquarters of the Jodo Shinshu sect of Buddhism, founded by Shinran. Jodo Shinshu is one of Japan's older and largest Buddhist sects and one to which my grandfather's family nominally belonged. By this time, in my reading and translating of my grandfather's memoir, I felt the word "nominal" to be appropriate, for Toshiro was not a religious man. He was an atheist but respected the chosen faiths of his children: the evangelical Protestant Christianity of my mother and Michiko, the Catholicism of Yoko, and the Soga Gakkai Buddhism of his son Hidero. From what I could gather from his memoir and Michiko, Toshiro had chosen this famous temple graveyard for its location and beauty. This ancient headquarters of his family's Buddhist sect also happened to be in the historical capital of the country and, as such, was spared the aerial bombardments by the Americans in the Second World War. Kyoto was old and beautiful.

The graveyard was carved into the mountainside in sharply terraced plots. From a distance, these plots looked like ledges with rectangular edifices of black and grey stone jutting up from the ground like miniature skyscrapers or apartment dwellings for the dead. It was a variegated skyscape, though; there was nothing uniform about the gravestones, some being taller or smaller, some weathered and nubbled, others freshly chiselled. The temple at the foot of the cemetery was a beautiful building surrounded by a lovely park with teahouses where you could sit and enjoy the cherry blossoms in spring. As we climbed up the hillside on a series of switchback stone steps, we got increasingly spectacular views of the city spread out below us.

My grandfather's gravestone was on a narrow ledge with a few others densely packed beside it; it was newer looking since he'd died just over a decade before, and this graveyard was in a city almost a thousand years old. I could see the names chiselled onto the stones: Toshiro and Kiyoko Saito.

Of my grandmother Kiyoko, I had little memory; she died when I was very young.

Michiko explained, however, that when my grandmother died, half of her remains were interred here and the other half interred at the head temple of her family's Buddhist sect in Nagano. When my grandfather died much later, his remains were initially interred in the Kyoto plot as he'd intended. However, some years later, my uncle wished to remove the remains to a new Soga Gakkai cemetery built deep in the countryside of Hyogo Prefecture in a place called Tamba. Michiko wished to keep the Kyoto gravestone in the family because she had many fond memories of visiting the city with her father to pay respects to their mother's grave when Michiko was younger. She offered to pay the nominal fees to keep half the remains interred in Kyoto, and it was agreed the other half would go to Tamba.

My grandfather planned for his death carefully. His instructions on what to do with his body were practical. His corpse was to be donated to the local hospital for research, but afterwards, the remains of the cadaver were burnt and the bones given back to the family for interment in the gravestone in Kyoto.

Visiting graves with food offerings and flowers—*ohaka mairi*—is a customary practice in Japan, usually done in August during the festival season of Obon when, it is said, the spirits of the dead come back to visit the living. It's a custom that has fallen by the wayside. In the many times I've been to Japan, I had never made a point of seeking out my grandparents' gravestones until now. In the past, I was too busy searching for other cultural traditions that would make me feel tied to my Japanese heritage. But this time, now with children of my own whom I wanted to connect with their Japanese descendants, I felt compelled to seek out their gravestones. I especially wanted to pay homage to my grandfather.

Before the visit, I bought small chrysanthemums, which are typically seen at gravestones and in Buddhist altars, and, after washing down the gravestone with water (usually there are taps with buckets and ladles provided), I put the flowers into the built-in vases. We had a moment of silence, then took some photographs. There was something in me that made me feel this visit was more than just "paying respects." It was not ancestor worship, exactly, but rather a feeling of deepening reacquaintance with the dead.

Not long before this visit to Japan, I had published an article in the *Globe and Mail* on my father's family's forced repatriation to Japan from Canada during the Second World War. My Japanese Ito cousin, Toshiko, had put the newspaper clipping in the Ito family butsudan in Oiwake, Japan. "I did it for our grandmother," my cousin said, "because you told the story of her suffering and hardship in having to move to Japan after all she had gone through in Canada during the war." When I heard this explanation, I unexpectedly burst into tears, tears that told me that what I had done in writing these stories out was true to my *vocation* as a writer. I had honoured the dead.

In that article, I was insistent on the use of the word "exile" to describe the situation of my Canadian-born father, his brothers and mother. But the word commonly used at the time was "repatriate." The options given to Japanese Canadians at the time by the Canadian government were "dispersal" or "repatriation." There was no term in between for those beings who were powerless to make such decisions for themselves anyway: in this time and place, that meant women and children. "Repatriate," in its verb form, means "send back to one's country." For Shigeru Ito, my grandfather, "repatriate" was exactly the right word for him, for it was by his choice that the family was made to leave Canada—a land to which he'd been whisked away by his uncle Saichi to marry his cousin, a land in which he had trouble communicating with its difficult English language, a land on which he felt perpetually alien. By 1946, Shigeru was completely demoralized by what had happened to him and his family in Canada. Sure, his uncle Saichi had done for him the best that he could, but now he wanted to go back to his own family in Japan. The pull was strong. After all, where does one go when defeated in war? Back home, to mother.

I had some sympathy for the man's feelings. Strangely, I feel Japan to still be my motherland four generations onwards, in large part due to his action of returning. Returning yet once again.

Unlike the urbane city folk my mother came from, the Itos were more traditional in their thinking about gravestones and "final resting places." Saichi was an adventurous risk-taker in his youth, but he was still a Japanese man of his time, born in the Meiji era, imbued with its still resonant Confucian values of family and propriety. Although he skipped out on his responsibilities as the oldest son of the family in Japan, he would still attempt to recreate the same age-old hierarchy of the *ie* structure on Canadian soil. *Ie* literally means "house"; the ie system was based on the practice of primogeniture, whereby the first-born male inherited the family estate and livelihood while non-inheriting children left the household. The main heir was responsible for the care of his wife, children, and parents, as well as being in charge of the principal residence, where the family crest was honoured, and where the family graves were maintained. The main heir family, sometimes referred to as the "stem family" or the "main house," was the seat of family authority. Saichi's ie was based in Surrey, British Columbia, on land where he, along with several other Japanese Canadians, had settled. Saichi intended that his children, particularly the girls, be educated in Japanese and that his oldest son take over the family property to look after him and his wife in their old age. As long as he could afford it, Saichi would do whatever necessary to continue his line, language, and culture in Canada. By 1941, Saichi had, by and large, succeeded at this endeavour. His three children—Chiyoko, Jack, and Kay—were now all married, two of them with children, and they were running a successful strawberry farm operation in Surrey in a tight-knit community of Japanese-Canadian farmers.

As an Issei and an immigrant to Canada, Saichi had no qualms about his identity. He was Japanese. A Japanese in Canada. Fealty to his nation and family in Japan was evident throughout his life before the war. Ties to the main house he had left in Japan were still important to him. That was why he sent Chiyoko, his oldest daughter, to the main house at the age of twelve to be educated there. Initially, the idea was to have her placed with his wife's, Ei's, family in Gifu, with a childless aunt and uncle who ran a logging business there, but that plan did not work, and instead Chiyoko was placed with her uncle Sentaro's family in Sobue. Sentaro was Saichi's younger brother; he had taken over the Ito main house.

At the time of Chiyoko's arrival, Sentaro already had five children, including his oldest son, Shigeru, and there were many more to come (the koseki-tohon records indicate eleven). The main house in Sobue was now at the height of its prosperity, in no small part due to the financial contributions of Saichi, who made lavish gifts of money and who purchased land on his visits. It was during Sentaro's time that a large wooden gate was erected as entryway to the family compound; it was a formidable sign of the family's prestige and wealth. The memory of that gate would be forever etched in the minds of the generations to follow, including my father and his four brothers. They would approach it as children for the first time in their lives in 1946 as exiles from Canada.

One would assume that if Saichi's home had been in Sobue in Aichi Prefecture, the Ito ancestral family graveyard would also be there. It was, but not for our 'exiled' branch of the family. My grandmother's grave was in Oiwake in Mie Prefecture, within walking distance of Uncle Toshiyuki's house. Toshiyuki's family residence where my long-widowed grandmother, Chiyoko, lived, had effectively become the stem family I knew growing up in my peripatetic visits to Japan over the years. On those visits, I had no knowledge of the family history or of how our branch of the family separated from the main house. In fact, I didn't even know of its existence: my father never spoke of his extended family in Japan. When Dad and I made our visit to the relatives in 1980, we'd apparently visited this house. It was the house of the Lego structure in the entryway where my cousin Toshiko and I had that glimpse of the disabled man behind the *shoji*, the sliding paper doors, who was Dad's cousin. At that time, if there had been any talk of that formidable gate to the family compound, I did not hear it, nor notice it.

When our family arrived in Oiwake to visit the Ito graves, I noticed some changes to the Ito house. The main tatamied guest room in which our futons would be laid at night, and where I had lain with my mother on our visit there the year my father died, contained the large and lavish butsudan my grandmother Chiyoko had purchased with her Redress money. It had always been there before but I had never really noticed it. This time, I showed it to my children. A resplendent cabinet of black and gold, glittering with fixtures, it radiated a *presence* in the otherwise spartan room.

New to me on this visit, however, were framed pictures on the lintel of the Ito dead: Shigeru, Chiyoko, and my father. As the son who had taken over stem family responsibilities, Toshiyuki was now making sure the family dead were acknowledged in the room where the butsudan was, just as my Auntie Kay had placed her small gold-framed, black and white photo of Saichi and Ei in her musty butsudan in her bedroom on the farm.

Shigeru and Chiyoko were interred in a graveyard down the road. Toshiyuki explained that the area had been mostly settled by returning Japanese repatriates from Manchuria who had received plots of land from the dismantled air strip previously located here. It seemed ironic that this confluence of returning Japanese—those who had set out of the country thinking to make their fortunes in other parts of the world—had ended up in this prefecture of Japan where, not far away, was Ise *Jingu*, the Grand Shrine of Ise, dedicated to the sun goddess Amaterasu, from whom, if you were to believe such things, the emperor of Japan was descended. I'd known before that our family was the only North American repatriates in the area, but Toshiyuki told me that some of the families that came back from Manchuria set out again not long after for Brazil in another wave of postwar emigration. I wonder how they had fared in South America.

We approached the graveyard through a gravelly footpath in a broad, open area where there were evenly spaced gravestones. At the entrance to the cemetery, you could fill buckets with water to clean the headstones and fill the vases. Shigeru's headstone was an older one since he had died not long after his return to Japan when my father and his brothers were still teenagers, but my grandmother's was more recent. It looked almost new, in fact. It had been only recently erected, even though my grandmother had died thirteen years ago. The Ito crest, a flower under a roof, was on it; I didn't know at the time that we had a crest. I took a picture of it. The children washed the stone while my aunt prepared flowers to put into the vases. Toshiyuki had mentioned to me that in a few weeks' time, there would be a *houji*, a Buddhist memorial service, for my grandmother, commemorating the thirteenth year of her death, and I was welcome to come. This reminded me to ask him about Saichi's land and the talk I had heard of it from my mother. What did he know of it? Well, curiously enough, in November of the previous year, he'd received a phone call from the Inazawa City tax office, asking him if he was the descendant of Saichi Ito. "There's some land in his name and we would like you to pay the property tax on it," they said. Toshiyuki immediately refused. He was not at all interested in paying tax on land he did not own, or would ever own. He had no idea where the land was, what kind of shape it was in, whether it was farmland or city property. Moreover, he was a descendant once removed—Saichi's grandson. The closer relation was Auntie Kay in Canada but no one in the tax office would have known about her.

Saichi was technically an absentee landlord, and such landlords typically lost their land in the postwar land reform scheme instituted by MacArthur. *Except for those landlords who were from the Allied countries.* I don't know who told me this or if it was even true, but the idea sounded entirely plausible and, moreover, intriguing, especially considering the fact that Saichi lost his land in British Columbia because he was Japanese. If the land in Japan had been kept in his name because Saichi was a Canadian, this was truly ironic.

Toshiyuki speculated that the land was farmland, and if it was, whoever inherited it would have to farm it as well. And there would be little chance of anyone doing that, he figured. Farming was not easy. Toshiyuki himself maintained several plots on which he grew shrubs and trees for landscapers. He was well past retirement but had been forced back to work because his oldest son, my cousin Masayuki, had skipped out on his responsibility to inherit the family business. This happened in late 2001 when Japan's economy was in a prolonged slump after the bubble years; Toshiyuki's family was not the first to suffer this kind of loss and breakdown in the ie structure of rural Japan. It was happening all over. But in our family's case, Masayuki was only following the lead of previous generations. In fact, he was downright faithful to the tradition of the Ito "jinx," as our Ito relations had described it. Before him was my father, who should have inherited the family farm as the oldest, rather than his younger brother, Toshiyuki; Dad, instead, returned to Canada. And before that was their father, my grandfather, Shigeru, who left the main house in Sobue to marry his cousin Chiyoko in British Columbia. And of course, before that, there was Saichi, the feckless, prodigal gambler who arrived on Canada's shore at the turn of the century.

Toshiyuki had little interest in Saichi's land. To have the Inazawa tax authorities track him down was disconcerting. His reticence to engage the matter was clear; I respected his desire to remain distant from the affair. But I was still curious. It was likely the land was in Sobue, although I wasn't sure, so I asked Toshiyuki if he had any more contact with the main house. He shook his head. Years ago, he had broken off ties with them over the funeral of one of his uncles. As mentioned before, Sentaro, the heir of the main house, had eleven children, eight of whom survived into adulthood. The third son, Kaoru, had taken over the main house as heir. And it was his son who was the disabled man I had seen in the main house years before on my long-ago visit with Dad.

It wasn't clear what Shigeru was expecting when he arrived in Japan with his family in 1946, but things had changed dramatically at the main house since his departure years before. His father had died that January, and Kaoru had taken over. It was only a year since Japan's surrender and the country was in shambles. For Shigeru to show up at the main house with some vague hope that he could yet inherit some land and make a living for his family showed the worst possible form of amae, that Japanese sense of co-dependency on one's family. Of all of children in that family, the main house had not expected the return of Shigeru.

159

Communication during the war years had been cut off and it had been years since Shigeru had left.

Moreover, it turned out that Shigeru's departure from the main house was ignominious. Like his uncle Saichi before him, he'd brought shame to the family name, but in a different way. He'd fathered a child out of wedlock with a woman from the *burakumin* class, Japan's outcast class. His parents wrung their hands. What could they do with this prodigal who was also their oldest? Saichi, who happened to be visiting in Japan at the time, stepped in with a solution. He would take his wayward nephew to Canada to wed his daughter. In the new country, Shigeru could be reformed, and the marriage would continue to unite both families. Naturally, Chiyoko was not consulted.

By 1946, of course, this was all water under the bridge. However, Shigeru's arrival stirred things up. His widowed mother, who had never really forgiven Shigeru for his long-ago transgression, resented this unexpected arrival of five unruly grandchildren and their Canadian mother, on whom she never looked fondly from the days when Chiyoko's care had been imposed on her by her husband. This made Chiyoko, unfortunately, again at the mercy of her once harsh aunt, now mother-in-law. She wept every day and, to make matters worse, she was pregnant. Shigeru, too, was at the mercy of his brothers, all of whom miraculously returned from the war. As Shigeru was the last to come home and was also unexpected, at a time when resources were scarce, he owed his family a debt of gratitude he could never repay. His early death at age forty-nine meant the debt would pass on to his sons.

My father and his brothers grew up with their Ito uncles hovering over them, expecting them to conform in a way that was honourable to family expectations. For my twelve-year-old father, proficient in English, exile to a war-ravaged Japan with its traditional values was a dead end. He knew early on that by whatever means he could, he would return to Canada. What the uncles thought of this ambition, I do not know, but as he was the eldest, they must have felt he had some obligation to his widowed mother and younger brothers to do the best he could to support them. My father's desire was only to get out of a bad situation in life. His mother, moreover, encouraged him. "Go back to Canada," she told him. "Life is better there."

Second brother Toshiyuki was not so determined and thus more malleable to influence. When my father set out on his course to return to Canada, Toshiyuki was groomed to take his place. He would inherit the land his parents cultivated in Oiwake beside his uncle Minoru to farm it for a living. There, he would look after his widowed mother and be responsible for his younger brothers' welfare until they were ready to be on their own. Two of the younger brothers, Stan and Tom, would eventually follow my father back to Canada. Brother Takashi would go to Nagoya, and Hifumi, the youngest, would stay nearby on land in Oiwake that my father and his Canadian-bound brothers left to him.

Hifumi and Toshiyuki married their respective partners and raised their families on this land in Oiwake. In the early years, it was used for growing sweet potatoes, which were processed at a plant Minoru had built on the land. This continued for many years, until Toshiyuki, along with other farmers in the area, switched to growing shrubs and trees for landscaping. By the time I was old enough to visit Japan as an adult, Toshiyuki was making a relatively prosperous living at this kind of farming and was hoping to pass this business on to his only son, my cousin, Masayuki.

For years while my grandmother was still alive, Toshiyuki maintained some contact with the main house in Sobue. He was now the stem family representative of our clan in Japan, and in some ways the uncles perhaps saw themselves as guardians of this particular nephew, whose destiny they helped shape after he'd lost his father at an early age. For us in Canada, these Ito great-uncles were vague, nameless entities. I'd seen pictures of them in all the formal wedding photos of my father and my uncles, although I never knew who they were. They were just men in black formal kimonos on the periphery of the typical family clan photo taken at weddings.

The only one of my father's uncles with whom I had somewhat of a passing familiarity was Uncle Minoru, who had the adjoining piece of land in Oiwake, and on whose property the sweet potato factory used to exist. His wife, Haruko, was so bent over from a lifetime of back-breaking work in the fields that her body was literally in the shape of a right angle.

If Toshiyuki felt beholden to any of his uncles, Minoru was the likeliest. There was a real bond of kinship and affection between the two clans as they eked their living out of the soil in Oiwake. But as for the other uncles, Toshiyuki felt no such obligation. So when, out of the blue in the late 1990s, his uncle Masaru in Nagoya called to ask him to dole out $20,000 for the funeral expenses of his brother Noboru, who had died of cancer with no heir, Toshiyuki refused.

And thus ended Toshiyuki's contact with the main house. Until, all of a sudden, the issue of Saichi's land came welling up from the past.

My arrival in Japan coincided with that of my cousin Fumiko, Toshiyuki's oldest daughter. Fumiko had been living in Canada for over a decade. She got her citizenship card in 1994 because she was a direct descendant of a Canadian citizen, her Surrey-born father. The Redress settlement of 1988 allowed children of exiles the option of becoming Canadian citizens. Fumiko, who had grown up with stories of Canada told to her by our grandmother, yearned to go there. After high school, she made successive trips to Canada and, with our family's help in Edmonton, settled in Vancouver. In 2005, she met a Canadian man whom she married the following year. Ever cognizant of the reason why she immigrated to Canada, she chose to have her wedding at St. Helen's Anglican Church in

Surrey, not far from where Saichi Ito's clan had its beginnings in Canada before the war. This was the church with the spooky grave-yard that my grandmother and Auntie Kay remembered running through when they were young women.

Fumiko's new husband, Robert, had gotten a job in Nagoya—a short-term contract teaching English. Although it was Fumiko's intent never to move back to Japan, she was suddenly thrust into the position of having to return. Because she was no longer a Japa-nese citizen, she now, ironically, had to go Japan as the dependent of a Canadian on a work visa. In following her husband to Japan against her deepest wish to stay in Canada, Fumiko's movements resembled our grandmother's.

Fumiko and I visited her parents in Oiwake at the same time. Aware that I was researching the family history, she offered to help, especially with some documents at the house that pertained to Redress and our family's history in Canada. I told Fumiko about Saichi's land. She became curious, especially as the land was pur-portedly near Nagoya, where she and Robert were currently set-tling. Her father, Toshiyuki, however, had few details. He'd abruptly cut off the conversation with the Inazawa tax office because he didn't want to pay the fees.

However, as it turned out, the Inazawa tax office did not stop with him. They then went on to the next brother, my uncle Hifumi, who lived down the road from Toshiyuki.

I decided to pay Hifumi a visit. It was a short walk to his house, down a road that went past Toshiyuki's nursery and rows of well-groomed green tea shrubs and the graveyard I had just visited ear-lier. The road joined up with an old highway that used to have heavy truck traffic. Hifumi and his wife, Sumiko, lived in a house right by the road. In my earlier visits to the house when their kids were small, Hifumi would give me drinks from the vending machine parked in front of the house meant for truckers driving through the night.

When I arrived at Hifumi's, he showed me a letter he'd received from the Inazawa tax office. The land in question was considerable. There were six plots, totaling 3,000 square metres. Four plots were zoned agricultural, one plot was zoned rice paddy, and the other zoned residential. The rice paddy and the agricultural-zoned plots seemed to be adjoining or close to one another, according to the coordinates, while the residential-zoned plot was at a remove. The letter confirmed that the land was near the main house, as the coordinates contained the name of the town, Sobue, which had recently been absorbed into the city of Inazawa.

Hifumi speculated that because there were so many plots, the city tax office had felt it worth their while to track down anyone who could make the payment. But paying the tax would not entitle the payer to the land. That involved the more complex process of transfer of title. However, because Auntie Kay in Calgary was still alive and was Saichi's daughter, she could potentially lay claim to the land and then will it to whomever she wanted. Unlike Toshiyuki, Hifumi felt there was some value to pursuing the land because there was so much of it and because a direct descendant of the owner was still alive.

With this letter, we now had something tangible to work with. There was an official attached to the case, coincidentally named Ito, whom we could call. Hifumi, however, did not want to phone. He was reticent insofar as he did not want the tax office to think he was interested in the land in case they might hound him for the tax. He himself had no desire for any more land than he presently owned, but he did feel, however, that it would be a waste to have Saichi's land taken over by the city because of non-payment of property tax. It had remained in the Ito family for almost a hundred years; was there not any way that it could be saved, especially while Auntie Kay was still alive?

Hifumi asked if I could intervene. As an outsider from Canada, I could make queries without implicating myself. I also was in contact with Auntie Kay in Calgary. She lived with my Uncle Stan, Hifumi's brother, and his wife, Happy. The other brother, my

Uncle Tom, who lived in Brantford, Ontario, was in charge of Auntie Kay's financial affairs. Hifumi had considered discussing the matter of Saichi's land with Tom, but the last time they talked, the phone connection was so bad, he decided to leave the matter for another time. Now that I was here writing a book on the family history, he felt that time had clearly come.

With my copy of Hifumi's letter, I used Google Earth to find the land. It was clearly in a rural locale but within easy commuter distance of Nagoya. Unfortunately, I couldn't pinpoint the plots exactly. I was curious about the residential-zoned land. Was there a house on it, and, if so, what did it look like? I imagined a house in the countryside: a long wooden bungalow with tatamied rooms and alcoves and *fusuma* sliding doors. There might be a bathroom with an old tub heated by wood. Around the house would be paddies from which you would hear the croaking of frogs.

I wondered if the house in Sobue on Saichi's land could be repaired. Over the years, members of my family travelled often to Japan. What if there was a place we could all go to? A place where we wouldn't feel like we were imposing on our relatives? An Ito house in Japan for the Canadian branch of the family?

It was a grand vision. Perhaps too grand.

I called Uncle Tom in Brantford. He agreed to contact the Inazawa tax office and talk to Ito-san, who had sent the letter to Hifumi. In the meanwhile, he told me, he would be visiting Calgary for Auntie Kay's ninety-third birthday in May and could, if things progressed from my end, discuss the issue of the land with her. He agreed with Hifumi that it would be better to resolve the issue of Saichi's land while she was still alive, since passing the problem onto the next generation of heirs would really complicate things.

Tom was also going to Calgary to settle Auntie Kay's financial affairs—in particular, her power of attorney. My mother previously had this right because Auntie Kay used to live in Sherwood Park. However, it had not been transferred to my aunt in Calgary, who was now looking after Auntie Kay's daily finances. Tom told me that the family had looked into Auntie Kay's inheriting the land several years ago, but there had been a problem with name changes. Auntie Kay had married twice, having been widowed at an early age. Her first marriage had been noted in the family register in Japan, but her second marriage had not. The authorities of the time needed proof that Auntie Kay had once been an Ito and the daughter of Saichi in order to allow her the possibility of inheriting her father's land. Since no one in Canada really cared about the land anymore, the issue was dropped. Dad died in 1990; then Jack and Chiyoko in 1994. Now, only Auntie Kay was left. I wondered if the problem of the name change would be an issue now. If the tax office was so keen on getting money from any branch of the family, perhaps they might be easy on the regulations regarding proof of identity in this case?

My grandmother's houji was a couple of weeks away. I would see all my Ito kin then and would discuss the matter with them accordingly.

In Japan, according to Buddhist tradition, memorial services are held for the dead every odd year: the first, third, and so on, usually culminating at thirteenth. This year was the thirteenth anniversary of my grandmother's death. By unusual coincidence, I was in Japan for this memorial. It would be the first time any Canadian member of the family would be in attendance.

By now, I had settled with my family into a dormitory in the countryside near Otsu in Shiga Prefecture. In order to get to Oiwake, I would have to take two trains, switching midway, to arrive at the closest station, Kameyama. Uncle Toshiyuki would pick me up there.

All was uneventful until I arrived at my transfer station, Tsuge. When I got off, train officials there informed me construction was going on further down the line and there were no more trains running until hours later. I called my aunt on my cell phone and asked her what to do. In my confusion, I told her I was at Kameyama. She told me she'd send Uncle Toshiyuki to pick me up. I hung up. Then I noticed the sign at the station: "Tsuge," it read. In a panic, I called my aunt back. By this time, my aunt had already instructed my uncle to pick me up at Kameyama. She had no idea where Tsuge was. She suggested then that I just take a cab, as the last call she had made to my uncle on his cell had gone unanswered. A cab! That was going to be expensive.

Tsuge was a sleepy country terminal with hardly any travellers around. Across from the exit was a white shack with "taxi" written on it beside an empty parking lot. Obviously, the taxi that had been there had left already, no doubt with passengers similarly inconvenienced.

A few feet away, a woman in her mid-to-late thirties with dark hair spoke into her cell phone. She didn't look particularly Japanese; something about her seemed foreign, even though she had otherwise Asian features. I went up to her and addressed her in English. She shook her head; no, she did not understand. Then I spoke to her in Japanese. Her face lit up in some recognition. "*Sukoshi hanashimasu*," she said, "I speak a little." Something about the accent made me realize immediately that she was a Brazilian Nikkei. She, too, was on her way to Kameyama to meet a friend who also did not know where Tsuge was. Perhaps we could take a cab together, I suggested. Just then, a taxi drove up. The driver, a friendly man, told us he'd drive us to Kameyama for fifty dollars. It would not be a long ride, maybe twenty minutes along the highway. That suited us fine; we would be there in time to meet our respective parties.

The cab driver told us that every second Saturday, there was construction and the trains stopped running. Tsuge was a small station that did not see much rail traffic on weekends, so closure on Saturdays was the norm. We visitors had unfortunately been caught unaware. The cab driver asked us where we were from. The woman was from Brazil, as I'd suspected. When I replied I was from Canada, the driver asked why I was there and where I had learned Japanese. I wondered why he didn't ask the other woman any questions. Her Japanese wasn't very good, that was true, but wasn't he interested in her as a foreigner as well? The driver asked me if I was here alone and I said, no, I was with my family, and at this point, the woman beside me spoke up. "I have a child, too," she said, flipping open her cell phone to show me a picture of her daughter, a lovely six-year-old girl with black hair. Her daughter had been born in Japan, but she'd sent her back to her grandmother's in Brazil. The woman explained how she had been in Japan ten years, working odd jobs in Tokyo at first, and now in the Kansai area.

I wondered why her Japanese wasn't better after a decade in the country. But she was a third-generation Japanese Brazilian and had grown up speaking Portuguese. In the last two decades, there had been a lot of Japanese Brazilians coming to Japan. Known as "*dekasegi rodosha,*" they were, in effect, a migrant labour force. Japan had created a special visa to be used by people of Japanese heritage in other countries to enter Japan, unimpeded, for work, or study. At the turn of the century, the tide of emigration out of Japan flowed in two streams: one to North America and one to South America, mostly to Brazil. There was also a second tide of emigration out to South America in the postwar period, but, despite these migrations, the Brazilian Japanese were never able to be successful economically in the same way their North American counterparts had; and, unlike Japanese Canadians and Americans who had the cathartic experience of the Second World War to cement their identity as North Americans, the Brazilian Japanese were still umbilically connected to Japan. Thousands would come over to work in Japan during the height of the bubble economy.

This woman was one of those dekasegi rodosha who worked at Japan's lowest paying jobs in its restaurants and factories, saving up money and sending it home. Her companions would form their own communities, enclaves of Portuguese-speaking Nikkei in factory towns like Kameyama, where there was a huge Sharp factory churning out flat-screen TVs. They would be looked down upon by the Japanese, who were not impressed by their work ethic and their Latino-inspired seize-the-day way of life. They would fill the pews of Japan's lonely Catholic and Pentecostal churches with an old migrant worker misery reminiscent of the days before Communism.

This woman's lot in life, so different from mine, hinged on a choice our ancestors made long ago. By the time I got out of the taxi at Kameyama to receive a warm welcome from my uncle, I understood how lucky I was that Saichi had chosen Canada.

I had never been to a houji before. To my Christian family, the rite was unfamiliar. In Canada, Dad had been an unobservant Buddhist and tolerated my mother's pietistic Christianity that set the tone of our household. Being a Japanese Christian meant stiffly separating oneself from anything Buddhist in ritual or form. As a Christian raised in Canada, however, I hardly felt Buddhism to be a threat. Most Japanese, like my Ito kin, were thoroughgoing moderns in that they hardly felt the need to be 'religious' in any pious sense of the word, but they did believe in honouring the dead. It was a strong, primal impulse and one, if I looked at myself closely enough, I shared, too. How else to explain my continuous pilgrimages to Japan if not in some opaque homage to those who left these shores long ago?

In some ways, my grandmother was calling me home.

The night before the houji, Fumiko, Toshiko and their husbands arrived at Oiwake from Nagoya. The sisters helped me go through a file folder at the house containing Redress documents. In it, we found my grandmother's passport—she was a child in the photo—and she was, at that time, considered a British subject. This would have been the passport she used to go to Japan for her years of schooling at the main house. There were also several letters from my father to his brothers in Japan—Hifumi, Toshiyuki, and Takashi—about the procedure required to file for Redress. The letters were dated, curiously enough, eighteen years ago to the month we were currently in, April 1989. The following April, my father had died unexpectedly of a heart attack during my visit to the house with my mother and Auntie Kay. April was also the month my grandmother had died, too, in 1994. Clearly, the month was of significance for our family dead. In addition to the letters, my father enclosed two documents of vital importance: a copy of the Ito family register going back to Saichi's birth, and a copy of Auntie Kay's application for Redress. The latter document clearly indicated that Auntie Kay was formerly an Ito and, therefore, Saichi's daughter.

"This may be all the proof we need to get things going for Saichi's land," I said to Fumiko.

The houji was held in the main tatami room of the house in front of the butsudan. A series of purple floor cushions, *zabuton*, had been laid in successive rows with the one for the Buddhist priest placed squarely in front of the altar where he would intone the sutras. In the alcove beside the butsudan hung one of my late grandmother's favourite scrolls. In her seventies, she had made a pilgrimage to the famed eighty-eight Buddhist temples in Shikoku on a bus tour for seniors and had received a stamp from each. This document my aunt Mariko had framed and finished as a scroll. Below it on the alcove shelf was a beautiful ikebana flower arrangement. These kind and thoughtful gestures Aunt Mariko had executed to prepare the room touched me; she was doing them in the memory of her mother-in-law with whom living all these years must have been difficult. She admirably bore the duties of the wife of the chonan, or the oldest son, and now that she and Toshiyuki were getting older, they were more aware of their position as the head of our clan's house in Japan, even though their son had departed and the observance of the traditional ie concept would end with Toshiyuki.

As this was the thirteenth anniversary houji, there were not many in attendance. My Aunt Mariko had invited some of her neighbouring relations, and there was Minoru's son and wife who came from the adjoining farm (Minoru and his hunched-over wife, Haruko, were both dead), my Uncle Hifumi and his wife, and then us cousins—myself, Fumiko, and Toshiko, along with their husbands. Fumiko, Robert, and I were the only Canadians there. For Robert and me, this was a new cultural experience. Masayuki, my cousin who had left the Ito household, also made a brief appearance. The Buddhist priest arrived shortly after ten o'clock. The houji began with him. The men all sat in the front—most prominently Toshiyuki and Masayuki—while us lesser female relations sat in the back. After a short service in which the sutras were chanted aloud, both by the priest and ourselves, my aunt fetched the boxes of crackers and snacks offered up to the butsudan and served them to everybody with green tea. After some visiting, the priest went to the graveyard to make an offering at the gravestone.

It was mostly the men who went to the graveyard; the women stayed behind to prepare lunch. My grandmother's gravestone was washed and then sticks of incense were lit and new flowers put into the vases. The priest intoned a short sutra, clasping his hands with a Buddhist rosary.

Lunch was a sumptuous affair of sashimi and sushi served in large lacquered boxes. Low tables running around the perimeter of the room had been set up for each person. I sat beside Robert and we chatted about Canada. Just as we were finishing up, there was a sudden loud *THUD* and the room began shaking violently. My aunt Sumiko, sitting across from me, gave out a shrill cry and grabbed onto the sleeve of the woman next to her. "It's an earthquake!" Toshiko's husband jumped up. "Let's check the TV."

Sure enough, the TV was already abuzz with the news. The quake was a 5 on the Richter scale, and the epicentre was in nearby Kameyama. There had been some damage to the castle walls at

Kameyama but no other reports of injuries or death. Railways lines were shut down and highways closed.

The phone rang; it was my maternal uncle Gen in Shiga, worried about me. He was calling to see if we were all right. Gen and Aunt Michiko were at a tea ceremony in a lovely garden when the quake hit. After the ceremony, while eating lunch, they heard the distinct song of the nightingale, whose call is apparently a harbinger of quakes. Sure enough, seconds later the earth rumbled beneath them.

With the hubbub due to the quake, I could barely interrupt to talk about Saichi's land. However, before everyone left, I managed to talk to Hifumi and Toshiyuki about the matter. Producing the Redress document that showed Auntie Kay as Saichi's daughter, I said this could be used as evidence for a title transfer if need be. I also explained about Auntie Kay's birthday. Toshiyuki was again recalcitrant, but Hifumi urged him to at least allow me, who was here, a chance to pursue the matter, if only for Auntie Kay's sake. He then showed Toshiyuki the letter he received from the Inazawa tax department so that Toshiyuki could see more clearly how much land was at stake.

Because of the train stoppage, Hifumi drove me back to Shiga to Aunt Michiko's and Uncle Gen's place. Since it was Gen who helped me with my initial search using Google Earth, I asked him to show Hifumi how to use the program. Armed with that information, Hifumi headed home. He would look up the land himself and see what he could make of it. In the meanwhile, we would wait to hear back from Tom regarding his call to the Inazawa tax office.

The morning after the quake, I awoke to a strange sound coming from the lawn. I went to the balcony and looked out. There, on the farthest edge of the lawn, was a pheasant. It strutted on the grass, with its bright red head and green body, its long striped tail pointed towards the ground. Its cry, raucous and throaty, was distinctive.

Years ago, just after my father died, I saw a pheasant for the first time in the wild. It was early spring and the weather was cool. We were driving back from the cemetery where Dad's remains had just been interred. The graveyard was out in the countryside, northeast of Edmonton in an area of grassy farmland and aspen brush. Just as we turned a corner, something flew straight up from the grass like an arrow. It was as if the spirit of my father was rising up for all of us to see him, one last time.

The pheasant is Japan's national bird. Of noble bearing and distinctive plumage, the bird appears often in Japanese literature. The haiku season for pheasants is spring when males call out for females with sharp, piercing cries. How strange that I should see this bird again, this time in its Japanese context, strutting on the grass, a day after my grandmother's houji, and a few days before the anniversary of her son's, my father's, death. Perhaps it was a coincidence, but the beauty and synchronicity of such an event were too amazing to ignore.

When I returned to my room, yet another surprise awaited me. It was an e-mail from the Canada Council saying that a grant I had applied for had come through. Now I had the funds to pursue whatever leads I had to find out everything about my family, including about Saichi's land. A brief, fleeting thought occurred to me: What if the tax on the land was not that much? And what if *I* paid it? If all the Itos in my immediate clan agreed that whoever paid the tax on the land had the right to use it, then what would it matter to anyone about the title transfer? As far as the Inazawa tax authority was concerned, as long as somebody paid the tax, they were satisfied.

A few days later, I talked to Hifumi. He'd gotten a more accurate picture of the land on Google Earth than I had, and he confirmed my suspicion that it was indeed very near the main house in Sobue. Curiously, there seemed to be a house on the residential-zoned property. This got me very excited. So there was a house, after all. What condition was it in? Was it habitable? A satellite picture on

Google Earth could reveal only so much. Clearly, it was time to make an actual visit.

That week I called Uncle Tom. I reported to him about the house on the land and the documents I found in the Redress file at Oiwake.

"I think someone lived in that house," he said. "Shima-san, Kaoru's wife. She didn't get along with her mother-in-law in the main house so she lived separately from her. At least until the mother-in-law died."

As for the Redress documents, Tom had received the papers from my mother regarding Auntie Kay's power of attorney. I was surprised to hear that both my mother and I had power of attorney. My mother had agreed to relinquish her name, but Uncle Tom asked if I would let my name stand. I wanted some time to decide, until after I had found out more about the land.

Tom didn't think some delay would matter. Auntie Kay was of quite sound mind and health, so my having power of attorney meant little in Canada. It could, however, be helpful to my quest here. I told Tom I would arrange a visit to Saichi's land to take pictures for Auntie Kay by the time he was there for her birthday.

In a week, I heard back from Tom with some disturbing news from the Inazawa tax office. He mentioned a name I had only just encountered days earlier in my translation work with my aunt Michiko in Shiga. After settling my family into our dorm in Shiga, I went to Michiko's place every day to work on the translation. Of course, I kept her apprised of what was happening on my father's side of the family. It was ironic, but because our family was in Canada, my mother's side and father's side of the family were relatively close and everyone was familiar with one another. Over the years, as successive members of our family would go to Japan or members of theirs to Canada, both Ito and Saito clans would cross paths. Connections developed that remain to this day.

As time was limited, we worked aggressively, translating from morning to late afternoon every day. When we got to the part about my parents' wedding, I stumbled on this one curious reference to one of my father's uncles. My parents had married in Osaka; my father left for Canada first, followed later by my mother. In his memoir, my grandfather recorded the events of my mother's departure:

> Akiko's departure was in the autumn. All our family went to Nagoya to see her off. John's uncle in Nagoya suggested we stay at his home because he had enough room, but we wanted to stay with Akiko in the same place because she was going so far away, and so I had booked us a room in a hotel already. I heard that John's uncle was put off by the fact we had not accepted his invitation. He might have thought it would have helped us if we didn't have to pay for our accommodations. But this was not about money, but rather, about affection towards our daughter. I wondered why he could not understand this.

Who was this uncle who'd warranted this strange mention in my grandfather's memoir? There was only one uncle I'd heard of in Nagoya, and that was Masaru, the one who had asked for the funeral money from Toshiyuki and Minoru.

Michiko remembered more and added to the story. My mother had gone to Nagoya earlier and had been forced to stay at Masaru's place with her new mother-in-law, my grandmother, who'd also come in from Oiwake to send my mother off. Masaru had insisted that because they were now related, they sleep on the same futon! The next day, my mother regaled her family of how her new mother-in-law had thrown her leg over my mother's belly during her sleep.

When Tom had first called the Inazawa tax office, he'd left a message, asking how much the tax was and how long it had been

175

in arrears. He told them he was calling on behalf of an interested party residing in Canada. This time when Tom called back, he received a surprising answer. The tax, which was about $3,000 and had been in arrears only since last November, had just been paid off by a Masaru Ito of Nagoya.

For Toshiyuki, the name "Masaru" was synonymous with trouble. Sure enough, a few days after Tom had called the Inazawa tax office, Toshiyuki got a call from Masaru out of the blue: "What's your family doing messing with our land? I hear there's been inquiries made at the tax office." The tone was bullying and suspicious. No mention was even made that the tax had been paid. Toshiyuki feigned ignorance. He had not wanted to get involved with Saichi's land for good reasons. He knew there would be consequences and that those would fall squarely on his shoulders as his father's heir.

Later, Toshiyuki remembered something that had happened the previous summer that he'd forgotten about. Masaru had called, again out of the blue, and insisted he cut the grass at the main house. Toshiyuki was too busy and declined. But why had Masaru called *him* of all people to cut the grass at the main house? Toshiyuki wondered. Why was he again being targeted for obligatory duty to the main house on his long-deceased father's behalf?

With this land issue rising to the surface, and my being in the country researching the family history, the time seemed ripe to pay a visit to this uncle. While this was going on, I received a visit from a former student of mine who lived in Tokyo, named Izuru. Izuru worked for her father's real estate office and was familiar with property issues. When I explained the situation with Saichi's land, she told me title transfer was complicated and costly. There was the issue of inheritance tax, about thirty per cent of the value of the land, which had to be paid by the inheriting party, and this tax was successively levied. So if Auntie Kay inherited the land, she would have to pay thirty per cent, and then if I inherited it from her, I would have to pay another thirty per cent. There was the issue of other heirs signing off their rights to the land. Auntie Kay would have to provide evidence that her siblings were dead. Then, there was the matter of zoning. If the land was zoned agricultural, then its use must be for agriculture. And, if any tenant farmers were on the land, and they had used it for more than twenty-five years, they had squatters rights to it. There were also broker's and perhaps lawyer's fees.

"This is only worth it, Sally, if the land's price is high," Izuru advised. "Otherwise, you'll be spending a lot just to keep it."

I had money, but not that kind of money. And of course, there was the matter of Masaru.

"So your great uncle paid the tax?" Izuru asked, incredulous. "Well then, the land must be worth something. You'd better talk to this uncle as soon as you can."

Who of my immediate Ito kin had seen Masaru last? My Uncle Takashi's wife, Sadako, had occasional contact with Masaru's wife and still had their phone number. "You know," she told me, "when Tom was here a couple of years ago, he went to visit him."

Tom? That was surprising. I hardly expected that, especially when all his brothers here didn't particularly like Masaru much.

"Yes, I saw him," Tom told me on the phone. "He was the *nakodo*—go-between—at my wedding. I visit him whenever I'm in Japan. He's getting on in years but he's in good health. He did very well for himself and lives in a nice three-storey house with its own elevator. He was very proud of that elevator. I'm sure you won't have any trouble with him if you tell him you are from Canada and just want to know the family history. I should warn you, however, that he's got a very thick Nagoya accent so it might be hard to understand him."

Immediately, I thought of Toshiko and Fumiko. They would have to come.

The two sisters, in the meanwhile, had also located the land. It was within easy driving distance of Nagoya. We decided we would find a mutual time for us to see the land and visit Masaru before Auntie Kay's birthday.

When I finally got up the courage to call Masaru, I heard a high-pitched, yet grizzled voice that was at turns friendly and suspicious. I did not speak of Saichi's land although it was likely Masaru had that thought in the back of his mind when he asked me why I was contacting him when I'd never met him before. When I told him who I was and that I was researching family history, he asked if I knew that he had hosted my mother in Nagoya just before she left. Masaru's memories were frozen; he spoke of my mother as if she were still the lithe young bride from Osaka about to board the steamer to Canada.

Once he'd gotten over the initial suspiciousness, Masaru agreed to meet me. In fact, he became very enthusiastic, telling me that he'd take me to the Ito main house and the graveyard there. We set the date for May 18. It was the Friday of the weekend of Auntie Kay's birthday party in Calgary. Fumiko, Toshiko and I agreed I would go up on Thursday by bullet train and we would locate the land before meeting Masaru the following day.

It was raining when I arrived in Nagoya. Toshiko and Fumiko met me at the station. They had borrowed their father's van with a GPS system. Traffic was light; we were travelling out of the city on a weekday morning. Sobue was about a forty-minute drive from Nagoya. The land was flat and of mixed development; light industrial alongside tracts of farmland. There didn't seem to be a lot of rice cultivation here. Toshiko said the area was more known for its shrubberies and nurseries; the influence of that cultivation had spread also to parts of Mie like Oiwake. Gingko, cut flowers, and lotus root were some of the other crops cultivated in the area.

We turned off a main road into a residential neighbourhood of houses clustered together in what must have been a village at one time. The road grew narrow and twisted; Toshiko slowed the vehicle down to a crawl as we peered out the windows. The GPS system announced our arrival at our destination, but there didn't seem to be a house or land that we could actually determine was it. All of a sudden, I heard the raucous cry of a pheasant. My heart jumped.

"We're here," I said, absolutely sure.

By now, the rain had let up and the sky was clearing. The ground, however, was still wet and muddy. A dog was barking at a house where the name plate said "Ito," but there didn't appear to be anyone home. Around the corner, there was a Buddhist temple with a parking lot that seemed not only a good place to park, but to make inquiries. Just as we got out, Fumiko saw an older man with a shaved head, clad in grey monkish garb, watching us. He went back into the temple compound. We walked into the yard to the temple-keeper's residence and knocked politely. The man answered. Fumiko explained our circumstances, showing him the letter from the Inazawa tax office.

The man looked at the letter and then pulled out a detailed book of maps of the area. It was hard trying to match the lot coordinates on the letter with the actual sections of subdivided lots that showed up on the maps. The man went to fetch a magnifying glass. In the meanwhile, his wife served us tea.

Toshiko explained how there was possibly a house connected with these properties. Did he know of any in the area that might perhaps be abandoned or belonging to an Ito? At this, the man looked up and said there was a house nearby that used to belong to a woman named Shima who had died the year before. Shima was the wife of our great-uncle Kaoru, who was the main house heir. "Are you related to this Shima?" the man asked. When Toshiko explained that we were, the man said, "Well, the house was in a bit of a state." It was undergoing some investigation at the moment, of which he could not disclose the details. He could, however, tell us where the house was.

It was located very near the temple. Following the man's directions, we pulled up by an alleyway that apparently led to the house. On one side was the walled section of a residence; on the other, an open lot of untended grass. The alleyway came to a T-section. To the right was a spacious residence with a large open yard in front. The place was well kept and tidy. On the left loomed a two-storey building that we could see from its side. Its back end was facing the yard of the well-kept house. To get to the front, we had to jog towards the left where there was a pathway to the entrance. The yard was completely overgrown with grass, wet and dewy with the recent rain. The two-storey house was clearly abandoned.

"Where's the gate?" I asked. If this, in fact, were the main house, then the telltale sign would be the gate. But there was nothing aside from a shambling shack of a storehouse further down the path. Toshiko and Fumiko were now at the front entrance. The name plate by the door, made out of brown weathered wood, read "Ito, Kaoru." Across from it, fixed above the wall, was a video camera.

"That's creepy!" Fumiko said.

Toshiko rifled through the mail in the mailbox. There was a gas bill addressed to a Shima Ito and a few other items. Clearly, the house had been lived in and had only recently been left in this state. The front door was locked, as was the side door from the kitchen, which was accessible through a narrow cleft that separated it from an adjoining building. In this cleft was an array of dirty items, old boots, dishes, bags of clothing, and appliances.

While Fumiko and I wandered around the house and yard, Toshiko was on her cell phone to her father. Toshiyuki told her that we were definitely at the main house, despite the fact we could not find the telltale gate. But there was one other feature of the house that clinched it for my uncle: the persimmon tree. "There should be a persimmon tree near the front," he said. And indeed, there it was, hardly distinguishable, for it was gnarled and old, and since it was spring, there was nothing distinctive about its foliage. For my kin, besides the gate, there was one other descriptor for the main house: it was referred to also as the *kaki-no-ki* house. Or Persimmon Tree House.

So, we *had* found the main house, after all. And in such disrepair. But what about Saichi's land and the house on it? Or was *this* Saichi's house? Had there never been a formal title transfer? In all these years, had Saichi actually owned the main house as the first heir, even though he'd left for Canada? That seemed hardly likely. And there was also the issue of his other plots of land, those zoned agricultural and rice paddy. Where were they?

We took a walk around the main house. A bushy pathway led out to an open field of grass with a shack at the end. Small bits of metal framework stuck out of the ground like skeletal ribs. Toshiko said they were the wire remains of cold frames or greenhouses. Obviously, something had been cultivated here at one time. We walked along a narrow furrow of dirt on the outskirts of the house property where we could see other surrounding plots of land with paddies and greenhouses. Were any of these plots Saichi's? How could we know?

Again, the shrill cry of the pheasant sounded in the air. I glanced around but couldn't see any birds.

We rounded a corner that turned us abruptly back towards the other end of the house. Here, Toshiko found the property marker: a stone wedged into the ground that indicated the property line. Not far from it, leaning on the back wall of the house, were two fancy porcelain urinals, one for men, the other for women. Made of white porcelain with elaborate blue design, they looked like Delft china plates. Clearly, they were luxury items; only a well-to-do family at the turn of the century would have possessed these. And here they were, unceremoniously propped against the wall as if dumped there.

The grass and shrubbery at the back of the house were too overgrown for us to go through, so we returned the other way and headed back to the van. We went for lunch and then to Inazawa City Hall, where an older, stockier woman came to receive our query. Toshiko and Fumiko showed her Hifumi's letter and plied her with questions. Ah, yes, she remembered this file. When the city had taken over the rural counties, there were new assessments and inspections made of the land. Although she hadn't visited this particular area, she knew of the widow, Shima Ito, who had been paying the property tax on Saichi's land and the Ito main house land for years. Apparently, she had lived for a long time in the main house with her disabled son until she became sickly herself and had to have him institutionalized. When she died, the payments stopped. There had been no indication of who would continue to pay the tax, hence the phone calls and letters issued to my uncles. The information they had received on Saichi's land had been procured from the land titles office.

A fellow phoned from Canada, the woman explained, and we nodded, telling her that was our uncle. And then, right after that, she continued, a Masaru Ito from Nagoya called and said he would pay the tax, and from thereon in, the entire tax bill for all the Ito lands in Sobue were to be sent to his son.

To his son? We all raised our eyebrows. Now *that* was news. Clearly, Masaru had staked his claim on the land. But you see, the woman explained further, this Masaru is the only surviving sibling of that family and he has agreed to look after the expenses of the institutionalized boy, his nephew. The disabled one.

We nodded and then looked at one another. We still didn't know what land belonged to Saichi, but now we discovered that Masaru had taken on the responsibility of care for his disabled nephew. In return, of course, it was only fair that he should take over the Ito main house properties, including Saichi's, to pass onto his son. This all made sense and, strangely, I felt a sense of relief. At least there was no imminent possibility of the city taking over the land.

This still did not preclude, however, the matter of Auntie Kay's right to Saichi's land. If, in the future, Masaru's son would require her to sign off her rights to it, we needed to know which plots exactly belonged to Saichi.

The land titles office gave us a copy of the deeds. They were old, handwritten documents, which I could not read without the assistance of my cousins, who themselves were at some pains to make out the old-style kanji and lettering. The information contained on the deeds was the date of the purchase and the names of the sellers and buyers. From what we could determine, Saichi bought the residential-zoned piece of land and the rice paddy in 1907, the year of his marriage. The garden-zoned plots of land were purchased much later in 1930, from his mother.

Using the information from the deeds, we cross-referenced it to a blueprint we ordered from the tax office to locate the exact plots of land. They were very close to the main house, so we decided to drive back out to Sobue.

The residential1zoned piece was down the road from the main house. The lot was an odd shape; it was difficult to discern where the house was on it. From a narrow driveway we could glimpse some sort of residence. On one side of the driveway was a lot of grass and trees that looked like they might have been nicely kept at one time, but were now clearly abandoned. This might have been Ito property; it was hard to tell. The driveway led to a modest-looking bungalow with white lace curtains in the verandah windows. There was a dog dish with scraps of dog food lying about, although there was no dog. By the looks of it, somebody was living in the house. Was this Saichi's house, though? This particular house seemed to be straddling two lots, according to the blueprint. We went round the back end of the lot, hoping to gain access to the house that way, but abutting the back end of the lot was another one with greenhouses that blocked access to the rear portion of Saichi's lot. We could make out some decrepit outbuilding from where we stood, but we couldn't inspect it up close. Those buildings might have been a house at one time, but that seemed unlikely.

The house with the white lace curtains had to be the one we were looking for. It certainly did not possess that air of grand decay of the main house; moreover, it was occupied. This was an unexpected complication; Izuru's warning about tenant farmers' rights rang in my ears. Obviously someone was renting the house and this income was likely used to pay the property tax. I still had a vague hope that we might find an abandoned house that could be restored, but this hope was quickly fading.

After we established the location of the residential-zoned plot of land, we looked for the other plots. The rice paddy was just up the road across from the land we had traipsed through in our foray around the main house. We were surprised to find the paddy glassed over with water, rice shoots sticking out of it like spindly strands of hair. Obviously the paddy had been recently cultivated.

Then we looked for the garden-zoned plots. On the blueprint, they were three elongated, rectangular plots of land side by side. We found them easily enough down the road from the paddy: there were three greenhouses on them, in use, that looked like they'd been there a long time.

"Someone's been using all this land," Fumiko said, stating the obvious.

We stood there, dumbfounded. Here was Saichi's land in use almost a hundred years after its purchase and over forty years after his death in Canada. It had been cultivated through periods of migration, war, and family upheaval, a constant in a sea of changes in the life of the Ito family. In this very spot, rice and other crops were grown, harvested, and sold by tenant farmer to landowner in a feudal pattern of existence hundreds of years old.

The raucous cries of the pheasant pierced the late afternoon air as they had earlier in the day. I scanned the fields and sky for a glimpse of their bright plumage, but I could not see the birds anywhere. The sun was beginning to set and there was a pink tinge to the sky.

When we left and headed towards Mie, I thought about all we had discovered that day. Tomorrow, we would be meeting Masaru. What would we say to him? How much should we tell him about what we found out about this land of our mutual forebear?

At Oiwake, my two uncles awaited our arrival. When we told them what we discovered, Toshiyuki made some interesting comments. He confirmed that it was definitely the main house we had stumbled on with its overgrown grass and the persimmon tree. The last known occupants would have been Kaoru and Shima, their disabled son, and Kaoru's younger sister, Hisako, the diminutive little perons, infertile and unmarried. "But there should have been a gate there," Toshiyuki said. That gate was famous in the memories of all my father's brothers. Hifumi had even heard a story of how my father had clambered up its sides and peed from the top. His insolence in the face of such sensitive family circumstances at the time was remarkable and must have cemented in his kin's eyes how truly 'Yankee' the family was.

Kaoru and Shima had repeatedly approached other branches of the family for an heir to adopt to take over the main house, since their son was incapable of it. Our branch, with its six boys, seemed a likely possibility. They asked once for my Uncle Takashi, and later for Hifumi. On both counts, my grandmother refused. There was no way she was letting any son of hers cross that threshold of tears as long as she was alive.

Eventually, Kaoru and Shima managed to convince Minoru to give up one of his sons. According to Toshiyuki, this son had gone over there as a teenager and had finished all of his schooling before running away. He'd been there for almost a decade until someone told him that no woman would marry into a farming household like his, in which the wife would have to look after a disabled person in addition to the aging parents, and live also with a spinster sister-in-law. The young man ran off, largely in an act of self-preservation.

The last Toshiyuki had heard was that the son had been institutionalized and that Shima was living in the house alone, bedridden. "Then who was looking after things?" Toshiko asked. Toshiyuki shrugged. Maybe a maid, or home-care nurse. In any case, whoever it was also looked after all of Shima's business, including the management of Saichi's land, no doubt. Who knew what kind of arrangement Shima had made with the current tenants of Saichi's land?

The eerie presence of the video camera at the front of the house suddenly came to mind. Shima, in her bedridden state, must have needed it to see who was at the door. The picture of this sick, elderly woman, who had looked after her disabled son throughout the years while at the same time trying to nurture the son of her husband's brother to take over the family farm, was a story in itself, of tragic, almost gothic proportions. The son, through no fault of his own, became a family liability, hidden away even when I was there for that short visit so long ago in 1980. I would have never known of his existence if Toshiko and I hadn't inadvertently stumbled on him that night. This son's life, too, was unspeakably tragic. And he was still alive somewhere in Nagoya.

That Masaru had taken on the residual responsibility for this son's care meant, for my branch of the family, anyway, that Masaru was entitled to the main house property and Saichi's land, since it was likely Saichi's land had been used by Shima as income of a sort. As far as my uncles were concerned, there was no need for further involvement in the matter. The land, at least, was not in imminent jeopardy of being taken over by the city, and the income generated from it might still be used for the remaining heir's care.

All that remained, therefore, was the story. Though mildly disappointed that there was now little chance of my inheriting the property, I nonetheless looked forward to meeting Masaru. He was the only one alive now who could tell the rest of the Ito family saga from this side of the Pacific.

Masaru Ito lived in central Nagoya in a narrow three-storey house, wedged between others like it, on a road that resembled an alley. A spry, sinewy man with stubbled grey hair, he awaited our visit with great excitement. He was eighty-seven, although he did not look a day over seventy. He walked without difficulty and was highly expressive and energetic. His voice was high-pitched and he spoke in a thick Nagoya accent, as Tom said he would. He and his wife had prepared for our visit by bringing out picture albums as well as ordering out for coffee and lunch.

We began with stories of Saichi. Masaru was a boy when Saichi made his trips to Japan, and the friendly uncle, bearing gifts from abroad, left a warm impression on him. He said he saw Saichi at least three times or more during his childhood. Saichi was rich and generous. To show us just how wealthy he was, Masaru brought out an old accounts ledger he'd recently acquired from the main house butsudan. It was a rectangular book, bound by string, with entries written in dark *sumi-e* ink. He pointed out money received for a wedding: Saichi's gift was ten times the amount of the others. Clearly, he was well-to-do. Not only was he making regular trips to Japan and bringing gifts for the relatives, he was also buying land. We knew this from what we'd discovered at the land titles office.

Masaru heard stories of Canada from his uncle, about fishing for salmon, about the cannery they lived on, and later about the strawberry farm in Surrey. Masaru remembered that, on one occasion, Saichi brought his wife, who, as he explained, was Saichi's cousin from Gifu. There was also the time he brought his daughter Chiyoko to stay with the family while she did some schooling in Japan.

"My father, Sentaro, agreed to the arrangement," Masaru explained. "But it was hard on my mother. She had lots of kids already, three or four of them whom she had to take to school and she was working the fields at the same time. It was really a burden on her to have to take in Chiyoko like that. Chiyoko said she was treated cruelly by my mother, but think how it must have been for my mother to have this extra child foisted on her like that. You know, afterwards when Shima and Kaoru were looking for someone to adopt, my mother told Chiyoko to give them one of her sons and Chiyoko refused. And I thought, how could she say 'no' when my mother took her in when she was a child? She owed it to the family."

Something inside me began to churn. I felt the old burn of resentment my grandmother must have once felt. As a child, she'd been left by her father at this house, and then much later was made to feel obligated to give one of her sons to the same house because of that stay, about which she had had no say. This give-and-take of obligations and duties within a family was particularly Japanese; often, it led to feelings of pent-up resentment and frustration, especially for the women, who had little input into the decisions the men made with their lives.

We were only at the beginning of our conversation and Masaru was getting his digs in early. "You know, there were eleven of us in the family at the main house, nine of us boys. When our father died—he was sixty-four—most of us were overseas with the war. I was in China six years. I came back in April of 1946, and then Shigeru showed up that August from Canada with five of his boys. Five! No one was expecting them. It was a big surprise. Altogether with his wife, there were seven of them that just came back to the main house like that. It seemed Shigeru was expecting something because he was the oldest, but our father was dead, and Kaoru had taken over the main house."

Here, at last, out of Masaru's mouth, was I hearing of the legendary impudence of my grandfather, Shigeru, who had had the gall to show up at the main house at war's end.

It was on brother Noboru's initiative that the land he had bought in Oiwake, Mie, be given to Shigeru, to be cultivated on a purely subsistence level for his family. Saichi's land, at that time, was already in use, likely by Kaoru and other tenant farmers who could not be displaced. Shigeru's family, after all, had arrived in August; the land would have been mid-crop. So Shigeru moved the family out to Oiwake by his younger brother, Minoru, where they lived ever since.

"Now your father owns that land and cultivates it," Masaru said to Fumiko. "But you know, he wouldn't have it if it weren't for Noboru. Noboru gave that land to Shigeru, and to Minoru, too. Minoru's wife, that Haruko, she's always saying, 'That's all before my time so I don't owe anyone.' But you know, we owe our ancestors everything. Everything we own comes from them. You see this big house I've built here with my own elevator? I owe it all to my ancestors. It's their money, too, not just mine. So if we receive money from them, we should give it back to them, too, don't you think? I mean, even you being here all the way from Canada— don't you think you owe something to the ancestors for that?"

"That's enough," Masaru's wife chided him gently. I don't know if he was implying that I should be paying something at the family altar or if he was bluntly trying to get at Fumiko and Toshiko over the old debt he felt their father owed to Noboru for his funeral. Vaguely, I could sense a pattern of bullying that I would see in other places in Japan. One was made to pay or do things because one was *beholden* to the other; this relationship could become abusive. Often though, the intentions were honourable. It was clear Masaru deeply respected and revered his brother, Noboru, who was obviously a kind and a generous man. And so when Noboru, ailing with cancer and with no children, was dying, Masaru wanted to honour him with a grand and lavish funeral. Without compunction, Masaru forked out the $20,000 for his brother's funeral and expected the other brothers' families to do so as well.

I knew very little about Shigeru, my grandfather, except for the few stories I heard from my grandmother and Auntie Kay. He struggled in Canada with his poor English, and he was a frustrated parent. He had little patience for his boys and they were beaten. As a result, my father never laid a hand on us: the worst he ever gave us was a slap on the wrist or a pinch on the back of our hands.

To hear Masaru speak intimately of Shigeru as his brother was a revelation. He was much younger than Shigeru, but had been there at crucial points in his brother's life; moreover, he heard stories from his mother about him. Often Masaru used the words "*gokudo shichatta,*" which roughly meant that his brother had done shameful things. Shigeru was the classic *botchan*: the spoiled first-born of prosperous, indulgent parents. He was prodigal and profligate. He left home early, stealing enough money from the family coffers to subsidize his playboy lifestyle for at least a year. Although not a gambler like his uncle Saichi, Shigeru was a womanizer, which led, of course, to the ultimate of shameful acts: a child conceived and born out of wedlock. By this time, Shigeru had practically disowned himself and was estranged from the family, working on his own at a small parcel-making outfit in another town.

"You know Shigeru had a son, don't you?" Masaru asked. We nodded. He seemed surprised we knew about this. "Well, I was about Grade 5 when it happened. I heard this crying at night—'waah, waah'—and I thought, 'That's strange, we don't have any babies in the house,' and then I realized it was Shigeru's kid! You see, when he was out working at the parcel makers, he'd gotten himself involved with some girl from a nearby village called Matsushima. She was the fourth daughter of a cremator. Anyway, he got her pregnant, and just around that time, Saichi was visiting. He'd heard from his brother how much grief Shigeru caused him, and so he offered to help him. They took out an ad in the paper to track him down and then, lo, he shows up with a baby in tow! I remember my father, carrying that baby on his back to hush its crying. Anyway, Shigeru went and registered that child under his name, and then my father paid off the girl's parents—compensation, you know—and then placed the baby with another family in Kameyama they had to pay off, too. I never saw that child again until Shigeru died. I bet your grandmother when she was in Canada didn't know that Shigeru had a son, did she?"

Toshiko demurred, "Well, actually she did know. In fact, before she left Canada after the war—"

I looked at Toshiko in surprise; this was news to me. I had assumed my grandmother had not known about Shigeru's illegitimate child until Shigeru's death.

"I heard she didn't want to come to Japan," Masaru interrupted, significantly.

"Yes, well it was mostly Shigeru's idea." Toshiko continued. "She knew of Shigeru's baby and offered to look after the child when they arrived here. But he told her the child was dead."

"No, he'd been given away," Masaru said. No one knew what happened to him afterwards. As far as the Ito family at the main house was concerned, the child was *persona non grata*. Masaru's account of the story judiciously avoided the word *burakumin* and yet that the girl was from this outcast class could be inferred from the fact she was a cremator's daughter—only the burakumin did this kind of work—and that he had named the village where she had come from. The burakumin lived in segregated ghettos and were not allowed to intermarry.

How had Shigeru met this woman? I wondered, leading to more unsettling questions. The burakumin were and still are an invisible minority in Japan; one would never know one to see one. Their identity could be revealed only by their address, and if employers never asked where their worker came from, a girl from such a family might easily get a job as a maid or a domestic outside of their ghetto. Burakumin girls were not usually involved in prostitution, so it was not likely that Shigeru had encountered her in a brothel.

The other possibility was that Shigeru had *loved* this woman, and, breaching all social conventions and taboos of the time, engaged in a relationship with her. And if this were true, both my grandparents were victims of the social hierarchy of the day, that rigid ie system that forced young people to marry one another for family reasons when they were in love with others.

Saichi's presence in Japan at this critical juncture in Shigeru's life clearly affected Shigeru's fate.

"Yes, because he was here when all this was happening," Masaru explained, "he offered to take Shigeru to Canada with him to marry Chiyoko. Saichi had been a troublemaker when he was young, too, so he knew what it was like. This all happened in 1930."

According to the deeds at the land titles office, that was the year Saichi bought land from his mother. It seemed a curious purchase; all the other plots had been bought from strangers. So, at a time of family crisis, Saichi purchased land in person from his mother, who must have been elderly at this time and presumably living in the main house with her son Sentaro. It seemed entirely possible that it was Saichi's money from the purchase of this land that Sentaro then used to pay off the family of the mother of the unwanted child and the family that adopted him. Such a large sum of money would have been hard for Sentaro to have come up with all at once, and it seemed, by the sounds of it, that Sentaro had already given up on Shigeru and wouldn't have contacted him except on Saichi's urging. For Saichi to buy land from his mother meant the land would be kept in the family. The money would be used to extricate Shigeru from his circumstances and, in return, Shigeru would go to Canada, sponsored by Saichi, to marry his daughter, thus ensuring for Saichi a continuation of the Ito line in a mutually satisfying blend of his clan with his brother's.

In a world where parents controlled everything, Shigeru's and Chiyoko's fates were sealed that day. If the war hadn't happened, the couple would have stayed in Canada and raised their boys with no one ever knowing of Shigeru's indiscretions. But Shigeru's return to Japan changed everything. It would stir up the dust of the past in unexpectedly humiliating ways for Chiyoko, who had never wanted to return to Japan in the first place.

All, however, was kept under wraps until Shigeru died. When it came time to sort out the inheritance, the family record—the koseki-tohon—was consulted. Unbeknownst to everyone, the child's birth had actually been registered under Shigeru's name, which meant that he was legally entitled to a share of the land. Now, all of a sudden, the child, if he were alive, had to be located. It was Masaru who found him.

"He was in Nagoya, driving his own delivery truck for a living," Masaru said. "I found him hauling stuff for a small company in front of the train station. He was surprised; he didn't think too highly of Shigeru, that was for sure. 'What kind of father abandons his son like that and doesn't even look in on him?' He said to me, 'And now you come looking for me after he's dead?' Things might have just ended there, but I had to break the news to Chiyoko that the son was still alive and knew Shigeru was his father. Something had to be done, so Minoru and I, and Toshiyuki—we went to see him to settle things. Bowing our heads, we apologized for Shigeru, offering him what really was only a token payment for his suffering, about $3,000. He told us again what a poor example of a father Shigeru was—not in a mean or proud way, you understand—but he had a point there, so I said to him that now that we knew each other as kin, he could feel free to come visit me anytime as I was the only one in Nagoya. But he said no, he didn't want any more to do with us, and so that was the end of that."

In the intimate, enmeshed world of the Japanese family, Shigeru's singular act of transgression so disturbed the family honour that a *second* payment was made on his behalf. Three thousand dollars was no small amount of money for that time. It was unlikely that Chiyoko had that much money, so Shigeru's brothers—Minoru and Masaru at the outset—must have chipped in. Shigeru's indebtedness to the family was beyond reckoning. No wonder that, even years later, his sons would be made to feel obligated to repay that debt.

Shigeru died in 1954 of cancer. He was transferred to a hospital in Nagoya where Masaru remembered taking blankets to him. His mother, still alive at the time and living in the main house, rarely visited him even on his deathbed. Toshiyuki recalled with wonderment how callously indifferent she was to her son's suffering. "It just seemed so unlike a mother to be that way," he said.

Shigeru did not live long enough to see his sons marry and have children. His momentous decision to return to Japan after the war affected everyone around him. The family at the main house was put out; his wife had been brought against her will; and he made exiles of his children. All this at a time when Japan was at its devastated worst.

The repercussions of that decision reverberate to this day. Three generations later, we are still coming and going across the ocean as if in its wake.

After lunch, Masaru wanted to take us to the main house. Twice in twenty-four hours we traversed the same road out of the city to the village of Sobue. Not knowing we had investigated things already, Masaru explained how matters had not been sorted out yet with the main house estate since Shima's death. He did not know, for example, who she rented the land out to, and was currently making inquiries. By the sounds of it, he didn't even know which plots belonged to the main house and which to Saichi.

When we reached the house, after a stop in the village where Masaru bought flowers for the graveyard, Masaru unexpectedly veered off to the left. "I'll show you the gate," he said. "It used to stand in front of the house but it was moved."

The gate? So it was still here! The shambling old edifice of wood we'd mistaken for a storehouse was actually the famous gate. Standing back, we could now make out the thick wooden doors squarely in the middle of a roofed building that was big enough to be its own house. A table of grey, weathered wood was propped against the doorway, which probably contributed to our earlier mistaken assumption that the building was a storehouse. In fact, the gate was a kind of storehouse; Masaru took us around behind where there was a room filled with old bicycles, mattress frames, and lumber. A ladder went up to a loft where straw poked out. Somebody could have easily lived in the gate, a watchman or servant boy. On my last trip to Japan, I visited a monk who lived in a temple gatehouse in Kyoto.

In rural Japan, a prosperous farmer had a large gatehouse that was usually part of a walled compound in which various branch families of the main house had their residences. Perhaps long ago, the Ito main house had looked like that, but it was in such decay now that it was hard to imagine. Masaru had a key to the house, and we crossed the threshold—something our branch of the family had not done in decades.

If this was indeed the house I'd been to in my visit in 1980 with my Dad, it seemed much smaller than what I remembered. In fact, it looked less grand than even Toshiyuki's newer residence in Oiwake, which had been built when Fumiko was in high school. There was the typical front entrance ledge before which you removed your shoes that led straight into a tatamied room, at the far end of which was the butsudan. The ledge, though, had been altered. A wooden ramp led up to a lowered section of the edge that was covered with thick carpet. Obviously the adjustment had been made for a wheelchair.

The house, cluttered and dirty with the furnishings intact, appeared only recently abandoned. Masaru was almost gleeful in his excitement to show us the place. The decrepitude, the decay meant nothing to him. This was, after all, his childhood home. I wondered how many years had elapsed since he'd stepped foot in the house. From what I could gather, Shima had been estranged from her husband's kin; no one knew what she was doing in those final years of her life.

The butsudan was lavish and large. Beside it was an alcove in which, long ago, had hung painted portrait scrolls of Saichi and his father, Kyozaemon. Now all that was there was a small table with a framed photo of the dead Shima. Grey-haired, she looked grim, the tightly pursed lips wedged in the face like a scar. In front of the photo was a typical food offering of a large orange and a rice cake, as well as an incense burner and a candle holder. On an upright wooden plaque was inscribed her new Buddhist name after death.

So this was the *Shima* whose name had woven in and out of our conversation like a pungent wisp of smoke since I began this quest for Saichi's land. Who was she? No one had given me her family genealogy. Her life with the Itos must have been hard. From what I could gather, there was much to be disappointed with. She'd married the third son of a prosperous landowner, but may not have anticipated that her husband would become the heir. Becoming the heir's wife meant moving into the main house, where she would fall under the thumb of a mother-in-law who was already proven to be difficult and cruel. A few times, I heard that the

195

main house heir, Kaoru, had lacked in backbone, and thus he struggled with the classic stem-family dilemma: who to be loyal to, his overbearing mother or his abused wife? Shima found life so unbearable in the main house that she moved out of it to a house built on Saichi's land, where she stayed until her mother-in-law's death. This was the beginning of her stewardship of Saichi's property.

Shima and Kaoru, of course, were expected to produce an heir. But their only son, after an early bout with meningitis, became severely disabled. Since there were no other children, the couple pressed upon Kaoru's other brothers to lend a son for them to adopt. Minoru's second son went but, in the end, did not stay.

At some point, Shima cut off relations with the Itos, probably after her husband died. By then, though, she and her son, along with her infertile sister-in-law, were firmly entrenched in the main house. They were the last to live there and it was the remnants of their lives that filled the house now.

Masaru showed us around. In the son's room, to my amazement, I saw the Lego structure I'd seen over two decades before, perched on a glass shelf over some dated stereo equipment. It was a replica of a farm compound, maybe of the main house itself. Near the Lego, jammed onto a shelf, were a TV, a turntable, headphones, and a stereo. The little room he occupied here must have been his den, a busy place in what must have been a very solitary and lonely existence.

Masaru also showed us the room where Hisako slept, which had the only bed in the whole house, and a wardrobe with dresses still in it. He said they were Hisako's dresses, but I thought the clothes in the wardrobe, the things on the vanity, must have belonged to Shima. I noticed that on all the light fixtures, there were long strings with bulbous ends on them. If Shima was bedridden in her later years and could hardly move, then such long strings would be needed. Moreover, Hisako may have needed them as well, being so short in height.

The kitchen was grimy and filthy. Jars of pickles sat on the counters and on the low table where Shima and her son must have eaten. Just beyond, by the sink, dishes were stacked in the dish rack. There was a kettle on the stovetop and a soiled dishtowel hanging near the sink. The cupboards were half-filled with foodstuffs like teabags and salt and tins of nori. There was also an old car seat, the stuffing all coming out of it, propped against a cupboard, with newspapers stacked on it. The son must have sat in that seat when he ate. The kitchen seemed to have been left the way it was, as if the occupant had simply walked away the day before.

Although filthy, the house was not unsalvageable. Solid and comfortably sized, it had a functional kitchen and a usable bathroom. The tatami was in good shape. If I had the eye of a stranger looking on the place for its potential as a residence, then there were possibilities. But for our branch of the family, there was too much unhappy history here for us to ever consider making a return. This house, brought to such ruin, was a personal testament to the decline and eventual failure of the ie system in rural Japan. As I stared at the severe black and white portraits of Kaoru, Sentaro, and his wife on the lintel, I felt like I'd stepped back into time, through the back door of a family saga of gothic proportions of which our chapter alone, the Canadian story, constituted its own drama.

After our tour of the house, we went to the Ito family graveyard, a short drive away. It had been moved and looked very new. Toshiko dutifully helped clear away the debris of old flowers in the vases and helped Masaru put in the new ones while Fumiko and I looked on. As Christians, Fumiko and I eschewed bowing at the butsudan and the gravestone, but I felt grateful that Toshiko was willing to do this on our behalf. Masaru pointed out the names of his brothers and sisters carved on the gravestone. Shigeru, my grandfather, did not appear here, of course. He was interred at Oiwake.

By the time we went for lunch, my ability to absorb the Japanese conversation was fading. I don't know how exactly the topic of the funeral money came up, but it did, forcing my cousins' hand in the matter.

"You know your dad and Minoru didn't want to pay that money for Noboru's funeral," Masaru said.

"Well, yes, it was a lot of money, but the request came at a bad time, you see," Toshiko explained. "It wasn't that Dad didn't want to pay, but we weren't married yet, and Dad had to have money saved up for our weddings, you understand."

Toshiko's answer was brilliant. She played one family obligation against the other.

"I heard it was all Haruko's fault," Masaru said. "She never thought anything of Minoru's ties to our family. No, she didn't."

Haruko had died just last year. All I knew of Haruko was that she was the hunched-over great-aunt across the road from Toshi-yuki's. But at Oiwake, when the topic of Noboru's funeral came up, the story had been circulated how Haruko, when she'd heard of the amount of money being asked for, replied that giving such money for a funeral was like throwing it into a hole in the ground. From that point onwards, Minoru's household and Toshiyuki's decided to cut off their relations to the main house.

Soh desu neh, the two sisters nodded. It was Haruko's fault. How much easier it was to blame the dead! My esteem rose sharply for the woman who had the courage to face down the bullying of her husband's brother.

Finally, Masaru took us to the nearby village of Shinmyozu to the house belonging to the family of his brother, Noboru. Noboru was a Hibi, adopted into that family by a childless couple of that name. Although he was the second son of Sentaro Ito, and would have been next in line to inherit the family property after the dis-graced Shigeru, his adoption by the Hibi family had ruled him out of this succession which then led to the third son, Kaoru, inher-iting the Ito family estate. The Hibis were wealthy and therefore enabled Noboru to contribute to the welfare of his other brothers when it was required. Only Masaru could have taken us to the Hibi household; he was our only link to that side of the Ito clan, since it was his wife's sisters—now both widows, as Noboru and Yoshiyuki (Noboru and Masaru's youngest brother) had since passed away—who were living and working there. Since this was a surprise visit, no one was home when we crossed the threshold of the Hibi compound. Here was the dwelling of a working, prosperous farm family, what the Ito main house must have once been like and could have been if things had not gone so awry in the past. A handsome, broad gatehouse fully allowed for the passage of a truck into the interior. Inside the compound was an open-air area with tables for working with the cut-flower crops the family cultivated. A small garden with a pond lay just beyond in front of the verandah that acted as an entrance to the main residence. The family was not home, so we went driving out into the field where we found them working.

When Masaru introduced me, one of the women said, "Ah yes, Canada! I met your mother once. She came out here to visit with a little girl in diapers. She came with Chiyoko. It was so long ago, yes, I remember her."

That little girl in diapers was me. So Mom, too, had once been out here, long ago, on a tour of Dad's relatives with my grandmother. She said she'd visited after her wedding, but never told me about this particular visit she had made with me when I was an infant. How strange that after almost forty years, I would come here again like this!

In the car on our return to Nagoya, Masaru talked about how he planned to hand over everything to do with the main house to his son. It would be up to the son to go through the necessary channels to procure the main house lands—that is, if he wanted to, and whether he would do this or not, Masaru was not entirely sure. The process would be time consuming and expensive. They would have to find the renters of Saichi's land and then collect the rent and pay the tax over a number of years, and if they wanted to sell the land, they'd still have to do an actual title transfer from Saichi to Masaru's son, which would involve the complicated process of contacting Saichi's heirs and having them sign off their hereditary claim to the land.

Traffic was heavy entering the city, so it took time to get back to Masaru's house. While Toshiko drove and talked with the still voluble Masaru, Fumiko and I mulled over the day's findings. We had witnessed almost a hundred years' worth of a family's tumultuous relationship with its overseas brethren that day. And yet the ties that bound—and often chafed with constraint—also miraculously survived. Saichi's land was a metaphor for that. It had brought together a remnant of the fringes of the family tree in a unique quest.

We dropped Masaru off at his house. This was probably the last time we would see him. I, the temporary visitor, had been the catalyst; from here on in, there would be no need for the branches of our family to intermingle again.

"So what are you going to do now that you've found all this out, Sally?" my Aunt Sadako asked me later.

"I'm going to write it all down," I said, already composing the essay in my mind as if it were a letter to my Auntie Kay.

"Dear Auntie Kay: About Saichi's land, I have so much to tell you..."

EPILOGUE:

POSSESSING THE LAND OF STORY

Auntie Kay died at 12:58 p.m. on February 11, 2013. I recorded it in my garden diary; a big, green, bound book with gold letters embossed on the front: "A Gardener's Journal: A Ten Year Chronicle of Your Garden." As with all diaries, I intended to write in the journal every day, recording whatever garden-related material I could put in the book, even during the dark winter months. Oddly, I discovered that I wrote more frequently in winter, often about the indoor plants or outdoor activities like skating or sledding, than at the height of summer when there simply was too much going on in the garden to record in the mere four lines allotted for each day.

February was the kind of month where I recorded things frequently, but the year Auntie Kay died, I was busy and did not record much but the one line about her death. I was home in Winnipeg after having just returned from seeing her for the last time in Calgary. She died on a Monday. I had flown out to Calgary that weekend and spent time with her in those last few days. Shrunken and shrivelled, in a mere shell of a body, she had stopped eating. When I arrived, she rallied a bit by consuming a cup of yogurt. I held her bony, wrinkled hand and pressed my forehead to hers, and told her it was me, Sally, come to say goodbye. She murmured "Oh Sally" back in recognition.

I left on Sunday evening. On Monday, I got a phone call, saying she had died peacefully, surrounded by other family members and church friends whom my Aunt Happy, who was looking after her, had invited. The church people held hands, forming a circle around the bed, and sung hymns while slowly, breath by breath, my great-aunt finished her journey of dying to arrive in the land of the dead.

Auntie Kay died at the beginning of Lent. On the first Sunday of Lent, I was struck by the words of the Old Testament reading that morning: "When you have come into the land that the LORD your God is giving you as an inheritance to possess, and you possess it, and settle in it, you shall take some of the first of all the fruit of the ground, which you harvest from the land that the LORD your God is giving you, and you shall put it in a basket and go to the place that the LORD your God will choose as a dwelling for his name" (Deuteronomy 26:1–2).

The day before, while cleaning up an old filing cabinet, I had found a letter of Auntie Kay's. There was no date, but in the upper corner, she'd written the address of the first care home she was placed in after she moved off the farm. By this time, I had moved to Manitoba with my husband and young son. In the letter, my great-aunt expresses her loneliness and how she misses my son, and then writes of her efforts at trying to save the farm by getting information on whether a new well would have to be dug (the old one was being tested for contamination), and her attempts to subdivide the house and yard portion from the field so that the house built by her and Sanjiro when they broke the land could somehow be kept in the family. Unfortunately, it wasn't possible and the farm was eventually sold. As I read the letter, tears welled up in my eyes and by the time I finished reading the whole thing, I was overcome with sobbing.

Auntie Kay once talked of willing the farm to me, but, as I wasn't a farmer and was leaving the province, the idea was no longer tenable. I was sorry to see it go when it was finally sold to the neighbour. My great-aunt was the last of a small group of Japanese Canadians who initially farmed the Opal area; the others had long since retired and left for the city. Although, in the end, my great-aunt's attempts at giving me her land had failed, there was one thing she had given to me in spades, and that was her stories. It was her stories that broke the soil and tilled the imagination of that nascent terrain of my identity; she was Japanese in Canada, like me, and she told me everything about what that was like for her generation. I listened keenly to those stories; some of which I wrote down that went on to be published. Later, I told a few of those stories to my children. But most of the time, I kept the stories in an unwritten book in that library of the mind, stacked away on a shelf, waiting for the moment Memory's hand was ready to pluck it out. When I knew I was going to write a book about the family history, I saw the project as a memoir, only as a signifier of a literary genre. But what is a memoir, really? The French, from whom the word comes, would translate as "written memory."

Suddenly, in that period of Lent, I felt a push to *write* the memory and 'take' the land of story and possess it, cultivate it; take some of the first, harvested fruits of that garden to its chosen dwelling place. I decided that for the forty days of Lent, I would write the stories my great-aunt had told me and remember her through them. Each day, despite a busy teaching schedule, I wrote the stories and, surprisingly, the words came as easily and readily as meltwater down a mountain in spring; there was always some story, some recollection, some memory that could be evoked. The writing was spontaneous and unforced—it felt *pure*. Michiko translated the stories, and eventually we had enough of them to make into a booklet, which we gave out to family at the memorial service we held for Auntie Kay in the spring following her death.

Such were the first fruits of the harvest of my great-aunt's stories, and with them I laid the foundation for this book.

As for my grandfather, that meticulously detailed scribe of the family, he succeeded in completing his memoir before he died. Because of his age, he felt an urgency to finish it, as he notes here after a final visit to his aged sister-in-law, Fumiko:

> Fumiko, Kyotaro's wife, was lonely after he died. Looking back at my diary, I see that my last visit with her was October 12, 1983. Fumiko was already quite thin then and her back hunched over. She no longer could see me down to the apartment entrance although she seemed lively enough in her conversation with me. We parted at the doorway to her apartment. When I was down on the ground floor, I looked up to her apartment window and waved goodbye. She waved back in return. I did not think this was our final farewell but I felt a twinge of something in my heart at that moment. It was a colder winter that year than usual, so I delayed visiting Fumiko by one day. On Feb. 8, I posted a letter to her. That day I felt some pain in my body and had trouble breathing. I thought surely this was the beginning of lung cancer. Yoshiko, who lived with me at the time, was not at home so I was in a bit of a spot myself, being alone. That day I received a telephone call from Eiji; he told me his mother had died. I thought Fumiko's death and my own body pains might be related and was spooked by the coincidence. Because of my ailing health, everyone agreed I should stay home so I did not

attend Fumiko's wake or her funeral. Fumiko died at the age of eighty-two on February 9, 1984. All the generation of my siblings were now dead with the passing of Fumiko and I was now the only one left and this was lonely for me. I am now past the age of eighty-two, thus it is I am hurrying to finish this memoir while my health is good.

In the epilogue that follows his memoir, he apologizes for the mistakes he's made, and ends thus as any writer might:

I left this memoir as a record of my life but as I am still living, I must think of what to do next. In Shiga Prefecture, they recycle old milk cartons, and make new sheets of Japanese washi from them using the old hand-craft method. I'm going to have Michiko send me the directions on how to do this immediately.

As for me, I have told the tale at last, and end with a poem:

Nation of Birds

What if our only home were the air
And our wings flapping through it?
And time the space we lived in
And the nest, a current for our eggs?

What if there were no abode but
Shore or field, one day to the next,
The wide sky, the only true resting place
Made of movement and yearning
For a never-arriving home?

—Sally Ito

Acknowledgements

It takes a village to write a book. I would like to thank and acknowledge the people and organizations that contributed to the conception, writing, editing and publishing of this book. Writing friends who have helped read, edit or comment on drafts of this book are Margaret Macpherson, Erna Buffie, Donna Besel, Lauren Carter, Sarah Klassen, Dora Dueck, Maurice Mierau, Warren Cariou, Lucy Lam, Fiona Lam, Leanne Dunic. Friends and family who have helped in the translation of my grandfather's memoir are foremostly my aunt Michiko Tsuboi and my mother, Akiko Ito, and my cousin Michino Phillips, and with other translations of my grandfather's writing, Yukimi Mizuno. My cousins, Fumiko Ito and Toshiko Amaike, assisted me on my travels in Japan searching for Saichi's land. Akiko Mrsa helped with the translation of recordings I made of certain family members when I was in Japan whose story became part of this book.

I wrote of my father's family's exile in the *Globe and Mail* in 2007, some of which I refer to or quote from in this book. A translated section of my grandfather's memoir also appeared in *The Malahat Review* in 2011. Some of the stories I wrote about Auntie Kay that appear in this book also were posted on the now defunct Cowbird story website.

Misuzu Kaneko's poetry appears courtesy of JULA publishers in Tokyo, Japan. The three poems in this book are taken from three volumes of her collected works—*Sora No Kaasama* (*Mother Sky*), *Utsukushi Machi* (*Beautiful Town*), and *Samishi Jo* (*The Lonely Queen*). I acknowledge my co-translators Michiko Tsuboi, and David Jacobson. David Fujino's poem is reprinted from *Paper Doors* with permission by the late author's estate executor.

I would also like to thank the Canada Council and Manitoba Arts Council for providing the funding for this book. I would also like to thank the Sage Hill Writing Experience where I worked with Denise Chong in a creative non-fiction workshop. In addition, I would also like to acknowledge and mention the Landscapes of Injustice research project that has recently uncovered new information and produced scholarship pertinent to my story in the very late stages of the writing of this book. Last but not least, I would like to thank the team at Turnstone Press.